Praise for *3000 ...*

"Lisa Deam reminds us throu[ ] ern words of medieval pilgrim. .... ...c pilgrimage is mapped first in the heart, and launches us on a journey that deconstructs our comfort, safety, and autonomy. Deam's accessible writing and deep knowledge of those who've journeyed before us make *3000 Miles to Jesus* a welcome companion for all spiritual seekers who find themselves drawn to pilgrimage's narrow, beautiful road."

—Chuck DeGroat, Professor of Pastoral Care
and Christian Spirituality,
Western Theological Seminary

"In *3000 Miles to Jesus* you will walk to Jerusalem accompanied by medieval pilgrims. You will also discover an instructive metaphor for spiritual formation in our modern days—pilgrimage. Much like the Holy City itself, the journey invites the reader to consider incarnation and transcendence. If you hunger for a historical yet fresh perspective on spiritual formation with invigorating language to reframe our walk with God, this book will come as a gift."

—Kelley Nikondeha, author of *Defiant: What the
Women of Exodus Teach Us about Freedom*

"I can't decide if what I love the most about *3000 Miles to Jesus* is Lisa Deam's evocative description of the life and times of medieval pilgrims, or the way she skillfully relates their adventures to spirituality here in the twenty-first century. Either way, this book is a delight and an inspiration."

—Carl McColman, author of *The Big Book of Christian Mysticism* and *Eternal Heart*

"In this wise and gentle book, medievalist Lisa Deam ably guides us into the wonders and realities of pilgrimage. Furnishing our scrip with stories of historic pilgrims and insights of spiritual mentors, Deam introduces us to lesser-known brother- and sister-wanderers who encourage us on our own journeys. With beautifully illuminated writing, Deam invites us reader-wanderers to begin again, today, in the pilgrimage of faith."

—Laura M. Fabrycky, author of *Keys to Bonhoeffer's Haus*

"With ancient pilgrims as our guides, Lisa Deam's lovely book will be a wonderful spiritual companion to all who undertake the journey. Deam doesn't call us away from the physical path of pilgrimage but rather helps us see that just as Margery Kempe practiced faith by walking, the inward journey of faith is also a form of travel. This journey might call us to travel with our feet or take us no greater distance than our own spiritual landscape. When I put this book down, I was ready to start planning my trip."

—Christiana N. Peterson, author of *Mystics and Misfits* and *Awakened by Death*

"Lisa Deam expertly guides us back to a time when God's people put life on hold and set off on perilous journeys guided by faith and hope. As she encourages us to travel along with the pilgrims of long ago, we can find the wisdom and hope that we badly need for the unexpected twists and anxious unknowns of our faith journeys today."

—Ed Cyzewski, author of *Reconnect: Spiritual Restoration from Digital Distraction*

"Lisa Deam's *3000 Miles to Jesus* is a treasure vault opened up for us by an insightful contemplative thinker and historian. Along the path we learn of saints—of pilgrims. They remind us that we never walk alone; we walk with companions. I am paying close attention to Deam—her work, her writing, and this book in particular—because I want to draw closer to Jesus. I recommend you do the same."

—Marlena Graves, author of *The Way Up Is Down: Becoming Yourself by Forgetting Yourself*

"Who hasn't sometimes felt like Jesus is three thousand miles away? You are not alone. That is the encouragement of this honest yet hopeful book, inviting us to join saints of old on a journey as long as the Christian life itself."

—James K. A. Smith, editor in chief, *Image Journal*, and author of *On the Road with Saint Augustine*

"In a world filled with claims of quick fixes and easy answers, Lisa Deam offers readers a different route: the long, arduous journey of the medieval pilgrim, slowly making their way to Jerusalem. Equipped with modest provisions and robust faith, some of these pilgrims left extensive records of their journeys—their packing lists, their maps, their journals, and more. From the deep well of her study of medieval pilgrimage and her own rich life of faith, Lisa has written an accessible and winsome guide for today's pilgrims—those of us who not only long to travel *to* God but also desire a closer walk *with* God. This book is a treasure."

—Richella Parham, Vice-Chairman,
Renovaré and author of *Mythical Me:*
*Finding Freedom from Constant Comparison*

# 3000

## MILES TO

# Jesus

# 3000

## MILES TO

# Jesus

## Pilgrimage as a Way of Life
## for Spiritual Seekers

## LISA DEAM

 Broadleaf Books

Minneapolis

3000 MILES TO JESUS
Pilgrimage as a Way of Life for Spiritual Seekers

Cover image: Shutterstock
Cover design: Faceout
Interior artwork: Paul Soupiset | Soupiset Design


Print ISBN: 978-1-5064-6163-2
eBook ISBN: 978-1-5064-6164-9

Soli Deo gloria

# CONTENTS

## Preparation

## Journey

# Arrival

# FOREWORD

Being a pilgrim used to mean you knew where you were going. Decent shoes, a full pack, and often a few companions were all most pilgrims needed as they started on their way to a destination that they had clearly determined. Canterbury. Machu Picchu. Santiago de Compostela. The Kaaba. Rome.

Nowadays our pilgrimages are more metaphorical, not because we are less spiritual than our ancestors but because we lack their sense of geography. We no longer believe that we can fall off the edge of the world, or that monsters live on those edges, or that Jerusalem is the center of the universe and deep underneath it is a winding passage from hell to purgatory.

We also, I think, lack the medieval sense of the moment. They plodded and pounded their way along the road. The plodding, walking, sailing, camping, cooking, begging, conversing were essential. A pilgrimage was a long process and yet the moments of it were everything. Where is the "moment" to the nearest airport for my Delta flight? The medievals had no need to practice any kind of mindfulness or "be here now." These would have made no sense to them. After all, where else could they be?

Perhaps we also lack our ancestors' sense of place. They were all about journeying to a place that was more sacred than the one from which they came. And it was a long-term commitment. Sometimes a religious pilgrimage was an excuse to leave behind a crop that failed or a call to arms, even a disappointing domestic relationship. That didn't diminish the commitment.

Some pilgrims who we meet here, such as Margery Kempe, were honest in their seeking, settling debts, reconciling with friends in preparation for a journey. For most everyone, a pilgrimage was about desperately needing to pray in *that* place, to ask forgiveness in *that* place, to see what pilgrims before them had seen just there, before they die.

Lisa Deam, an expert medievalist and writer, gets at these contrasts throughout her book. "We're going all the way to the city that shimmers beneath a horizon we cannot yet see," she tells us, beautifully, at the outset, and immediately I wanted to go. My intentions on the journey are not always good, but I know that the journey is everything. Deam helps us see how that is.

Lisa Deam brings with her several other guides—medieval figures whom she brings to life in character and apt quotation. Some may be familiar to you; others will be new. I particularly enjoyed meeting Swiss Dominican Felix Fabri, who was terrified to cross the Mediterranean Sea on his way to the Holy Land, and due in part to his terror had to endure the voyage and its rats, storms, and chamber pots not once but four times! Finally, he saw the land that he had longed to see.

This is a journey for pilgrims, wherever we find ourselves now. Deam guides us in a way that combines the good literal qualities that we've lost to history and the beneficent ways of today's armchair version. "A pilgrim never walks alone," she tells us. Also, she reminds us to listen to other medievals like Dante, who tells us we are strangers in this land. Most of all, remember that your longing and your hope for God will lead you to that shimmering place you can't quite see.

—Jon M. Sweeney
author of *James Martin, SJ: In the Company of Jesus*
and *Nicholas Black Elk: Medicine Man, Catechist, Saint*

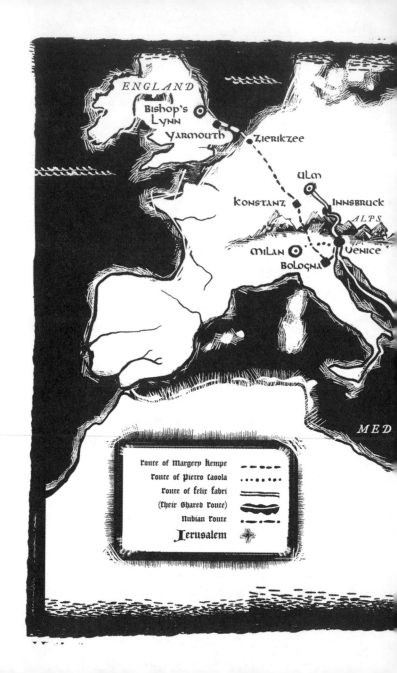

ENGLAND

Bishop's Lynn

Yarmouth

Zierikzee

Ulm

Konstanz

Innsbruck

ALPS

Milan

Venice

Bologna

MED

route of Margery Kempe
route of Pietro Casola
route of Felix Fabri
(their shared route)
Nubian route

Jerusalem

# FOUR PILGRIMAGES TO THE HOLY LAND

BLACK SEA

CONSTANTINOPLE

...RANEAN SEA

THE HOLY LAND

JAFFA

EGYPT

Jerusalem

ASWAN

NUBIA

RED SEA

# INTRODUCTION

A few holidays ago, my family embarked on a Great American Pilgrimage. We packed our bags, rose early, and traveled halfway across the country to be home for Christmas. At the airport, we joined thousands of other pilgrims making the same journey. It was the usual drill. We were searched and herded. We boarded and fought for luggage space. We buckled in and waited. After taking off, I performed my habitual duty and ensured a safe flight by clutching the armrests the entire way. Inevitably, we arrived late. Due to foggy conditions on the ground, our plane circled the airport for an hour before landing. Finally we touched ground and disembarked, and so eager was my mother to transport us to my ancestral home that she got a speeding ticket on the way.

I did not endure this journey with grace. Instead, I grumbled. I was indignant when my luggage was searched. I grimaced at the close quarters with all those strangers. I gave thanks for a (relatively) smooth flight only to become incensed when our landing was delayed.

Yet a good thing came out of this journey: perspective. My hours above the earth gave me a God-like view of the landscape and plenty of time to think. Watching fields and lakes slip into and out of view amid the clouds, I reflected on my sorry pilgrimage. As a card-carrying medievalist, I couldn't help comparing myself to history's *real* pilgrims—those faithful travelers who wandered the physical and spiritual landscape of the Middle Ages. Like me, medieval pilgrims specialized in difficult journeys. But there the similarity ends. Medieval pilgrims traveled farther and more often than I, and they did so with a stamina I can't seem to muster.

The more I travel, the more I admire history's premier travel experts. In the Middle Ages, pilgrims regularly went halfway across their continent and in some cases halfway around the world. And they did most of that traveling on foot. An English pilgrim going to

Santiago de Compostela, for example, walked nearly two thousand miles to a church that, according to medieval maps, lay at the ends of the earth.

The epic journey to Jerusalem was half again as long. If Santiago de Compostela hugged the earth's edge, Jerusalem lay at its very center. Before depositing pilgrims in the Holy Land, the road to Jerusalem led them through the Alps and across the Mediterranean Sea. This journey, some three thousand miles in all, would have taken, at minimum, three months— each way. When the English mystic Margery Kempe left for Jerusalem in 1413, she embarked on an Odyssean voyage of eighteen months.

To take these monumental journeys, pilgrims put their life on hold. To say it another way, their life *became* the journey. They lived and breathed and walked their quest for the sacred.

These pilgrims set me to thinking about journeys large and small. The metal tube that encased me while hurtling so unnaturally through the air eventually (God be thanked) returned to terra firma. My Great American Pilgrimage came to an end. But the sacred quest that is my life continued.

My quest continued when I walked in the front door of my mother's house to celebrate the holiday with my family.

It continued when I returned home (another journey in the metal tube) to the demands and problems of everyday life.

And I continue to live this quest.

I live it as I mature, age, and navigate the joys and sorrows that befall us in the land of the living.

I live it as I grapple with my faith, wrestle with doubts, and both mourn and accept the road that has been given me to toe.

I will live this quest until my final breath.

I don't just take journeys; like a medieval pilgrim, I live the journey. My life, like yours, is a long and winding road leading through the sum of our days. Along with all those pilgrims who went before us, we're questing for the sacred: we seek the divine presence each day and wait for God to welcome us at the end of life's road.

How will we live the journey of our life, including the myriad treks that make up each day? We can live it like I did on my airplane voyage, hurtling forward at a fast pace and enduring emotional upsets with every detour. Or we can learn to travel well and make a good end. This book is about traveling well, about learning to embrace a life of intentional pilgrimage. It is my hope that the historical wisdom collected here will help us live our journeys, both large and small, with the sacred meaning and purpose they deserve.

A couple of months after my Great American Pilgrimage, I attained a certain age in my life, one generally referred to as a "milestone." It unleashed in full force all the questions raised by my trip in the metal tube. At this pivotal point in my life, I became convicted that my spiritual journey more resembled an airplane voyage than the sacred quest I wanted it to be. There's nothing like a birthday to signal that one doesn't have all the time in the world to make course corrections. The *big* birthday screamed out that it was time to get serious about life's journey. So I revisited the medieval pilgrims who dogged me on that holiday airplane ride. As I dug deeper into their history, I found they had quite a bit to say about traveling well on life's sacred quest.

As I studied pilgrims' journeys, I felt prompted to live into them and to share their wisdom. The book you're holding is the result. Medieval pilgrimage is well worth sharing. These spiritual accounts and travel stories are part of the history of our faith and important for anyone who understands, deeply, that life is taking them on a journey.

I wrote this book for me as much as for you. As I researched, I discovered that in their travels, medieval pilgrims displayed qualities I wanted to emulate. They were patient. Faithful. Courageous. And inefficient—gloriously so. Pilgrims were in it for the long haul. They risked everything to take a journey of faith. And the conviction that drove them is one to which I daily aspire.

This little book is for anyone who, like me, wants to learn to travel well on the lifelong road of faith. It's an invitation to travel like a medieval pilgrim. To take this road, you won't have to give up flush toilets, warm beds, or cell phones. You don't even have to leave your sofa, if you don't want to. But the pilgrims with whom we journey do ask us to embrace spiritual risk and adventure, because we're walking a wild and wonderful way. We're going all the way to the city that shimmers beneath a horizon we cannot yet see. We're going to Jerusalem, the city at the center of the world—the city where Jesus waits to welcome us home.

We won't be walking this road alone. Each step of the way, we'll be accompanied by a communion of pilgrim saints, such as the Swiss friar Felix Fabri, who relished adventure, and the English mystic Margery Kempe, whose journey prompted visions and healing tears. These pilgrims will be our guides and advisers. Through their travel journals, they've shown us the way forward.

In this book about pilgrims' journeys, I've used the form of a travel guide. Each chapter explores one step of the medieval road to Jerusalem. As we follow along, we'll see how these steps inform our own walk of faith. Our spiritual itinerary includes some of the same challenges pilgrims faced, such as writing our will, confronting our internal enemies, and entering unknown lands.

There's nothing easy about this pilgrimage. Nothing safe. Nothing glamorous. In fact, it upends our usual way of traveling. It gets us off our nonstop flight and takes us on the most humbling road imaginable. Pilgrimage is a path that requires bravery on the part of any soul who undertakes this sacred quest.

But there's good news. The pilgrim who commits to the journey is assured to arrive. The fourteenth-century mystic Walter Hilton tells us that when the road gets rough, we should keep going. "Keep on your way and think of Jerusalem," he says. As we go along,

Hilton will be one of our guides, with good advice for spiritual travelers. "If you keep on this way," he writes, "I promise that you will not be slain but come to the place that you desire." These words alert us to the danger of our voyage but also to its hope. Heeding Hilton's wisdom, coupled with that of the pilgrims who wound their long and faithful way to the center of the world, we can complete our own journey and make a good end. Pointing our feet to Jerusalem, we know we will reach its gates.

Are you ready to get going? Grab your staff and scrip, because it's three thousand miles to Jesus.

# Preparation

LONGING FOR A BETTER COUNTRY

# I

# Everyone a Pilgrim

"In the broad sense, a 'pilgrim' is one who is a stranger," wrote Dante Alighieri in the early 1290s. "In the strict sense," he added, "the word 'pilgrim' is not meant unless the person travels toward Santiago de Compostela or elsewhere." For Dante, pilgrimage required two elements: the challenge of distance and the sense of being strangers in a strange land.

In the Middle Ages, every person en route to a distant site was, of course, a "stranger," that is, a traveler in a foreign land. Yet in the language of faith, the word *stranger* has a larger meaning, describing someone on the road of life—someone who walks in faith with God, someone who sets her sights on a future hope. This faith-based language echoes throughout Scripture and the Christian tradition. In the book of Hebrews, for instance, a stranger is one who does not make a home upon this earth but is "longing for a better country—a heavenly one" (Heb 11:16 NIV).

In this larger sense, all who walk the road of faith are strangers. All are pilgrims. We in the twenty-first century receive this call, as did seekers in Dante's time. To respond is to embark on a path that holds both challenge and promise. It is to go great distances, but not (necessarily) physically. A true pilgrim travels nowhere more distant than the landscape of her own faith. Remarking on the importance of the journey in our spiritual life, theologian and author Eugene Peterson said that the designation of the pilgrim "tells us we are people who spend our lives going someplace, going to God." Our longing and our hope make us travelers.

Few of us will regularly walk long distances as part of our faith journey. Medieval pilgrims, of course, did. They walked to Santiago de Compostela, as Dante mentions, and also to Canterbury, Rome, and Jerusalem, among other sites. As travelers today might be recognized by a backpack, pilgrims donned a uniform that marked them as adventurers on the road of faith. They put on a protective cloak, carried a staff for defense against wild animals, and hung a leather scrip, or pouch, around their shoulder or waist. After receiving a blessing, the well-outfitted pilgrims were launched upon the path.

Despite the rain and the sun that bore down on pilgrims and the dust that clung to their feet, these wanderers trod more than a physical path. For in the Middle Ages, Dante's two definitions of pilgrimage frequently intertwined. The road invited pilgrims to become both a stranger in a strange land and a stranger on the road of faith. One kind of journey fed the other.

Responding to the call to walk our own road, we can take these faithful travelers to be our guides and companions. They speak into our journey, offering to teach us about pilgrimage as a way of life. As we would for any companion with whom we're preparing to travel a long distance, we should first settle in and listen to their stories. And so, getting ready to embark, we meet with three pilgrims who set out in the 1400s to the Holy Land:

🌸 In 1413, an English laywoman named Margery Kempe responded to a charge from God to journey three thousand miles to Jerusalem. She announced her intention to depart, settled her debts, and raised funds. Her journey to the Holy Land and beyond took her away from her community and family for some eighteen months.

🌸 In 1480, a Swiss Dominican friar named Felix
Fabri, overcome with a "fever of longing" to
see the holy places, set his face toward Jerusalem. He made an oath, traveled the European continent gathering documents and
funds, and promised his brethren to keep a
record of all that happened on his journey.
Among the many fears Felix conquered on
his travels to the Holy Land was his dread of
the sea.

🌸 Then in 1494, an Italian canon named Pietro
Casola, at sixty-seven years of age, fulfilled a
desire he'd held since his youth. He traveled
to the land beyond the sea. In addition to practical preparations, he took care, as he wrote,
to "furnish myself with spiritual weapons for
my protection." Having found no companions
willing to accompany him, he resolutely set
off for Jerusalem alone in the hopes of finding
friends along the way.

The journeys of Margery, Felix, and Pietro would
lead them on an adventure like no other. They traveled over the Alps, across the Mediterranean Sea,
and into a foreign land that was both welcoming
and hostile. Some might call their pilgrimage a foolhardy enterprise. These pilgrims took with them no

guarantees of safety or success; they relied only on a scrip filled with desire, determination, and faith (and, yes, a bit of money). For each of them, these meager supplies proved enough.

In pilgrims' journeys, we find something of value for our own foolhardy enterprise of faith. Our three travelers were pilgrims in a traditional or historical sense, journeying many miles to a site of sacred and personal importance. Yet their pilgrimage taught them—and can teach us—about life's larger journey, which we, as spiritual seekers, share with them.

And so it is that pilgrims in Dante's strict sense help us to become pilgrims in the broad and arguably more important sense. While we may never take a physical journey resembling that of Margery, Felix, and Pietro, we have something to learn from them about our pilgrimage to a better country.

As our three travelers set out on a challenging physical road, they likely didn't think of themselves as stout or courageous. They lived in an age when people regularly took journeys of astounding length and risk.

This historical phenomenon—the pilgrimage phenomenon—can be difficult to grasp today. For twenty-first-century Americans, pilgrimage is simply not part of the cultural DNA. It may not be part of our spiritual formation, either. While those raised in Catholic and other liturgical traditions might be familiar with the language of spiritual practices and pilgrimage, these topics are largely foreign to those of us who grew up in the Protestant church.

Yet for many, physical pilgrimage is becoming an important way to experience or seek deeper faith. The thousands of people who today walk all or part of the Camino de Santiago, for example, are undertaking a decidedly medieval practice. In the Middle Ages, Santiago was the most popular pilgrimage destination in Europe outside of Rome. The Camino's network of routes led to the Cathedral of Santiago de Compostela in Spain, the resting place of James the Greater. Along with other historical routes, the Camino has undergone a revival in recent times, helping modern seekers better understand what it means to be a pilgrim.

As this practice attracts more and more interest from people of various faith traditions, there's a question we might ask alongside Margery, Felix, and Pietro: Why did they—and why do we now—feel this need? Why did these pilgrims, and many others like them, embark on foot journeys of hundreds and thousands of miles?

Sometimes, pilgrims' journeys were tied to a sense of desperation leading them to pray for healing at a particular holy site. Or they might be prompted by church-political teachings of the time, such as gaining indulgences from visiting certain destinations.

Yet pilgrims also traveled as an act of faith. In Geoffrey Chaucer's *Canterbury Tales*, written in the late fourteenth century, a fictional cast of characters travels to the shrine of Saint Thomas Becket at Canterbury Cathedral. Within the poem are pilgrim tales revealing a healthy interest in the world and its comforts. But as the sun sets on the final day of their journey, the character of the parson recalls the pilgrims to their larger purpose: "Now, at the end of our journey, I will bring matters to a conclusion. May the Saviour guide me and inspire me to lead you to Jerusalem. Our pilgrimage on earth is an image of the glorious pilgrimage to the celestial city." For a medieval pilgrim, every journey to a holy site echoed the quest for the heavenly city at the end of life's road. Physical journeys taught the call to be a pilgrim in one's spiritual life.

Pilgrims responding to this call had many sites from which to choose. Some pilgrims, including Margery Kempe, visited all three of the top pilgrimage destinations of the medieval period: Rome, Santiago de Compostela, and Jerusalem. Of these, Jerusalem held a special status and forms the focus of this book. Boasting an intimate connection to the life and death of Christ, Jerusalem gave its visitors the opportunity to follow in the footsteps of their Lord. Pilgrims prayed in the landscape where Jesus taught and healed; they wept at the site of Calvary, where he suffered; they rejoiced at the empty tomb, where he rose again. And they learned about the path of the Christian life through the difficulties of their long journey to the sacred city. As we follow the Jerusalem path, we can learn from the discipleship and spiritual discipline of pilgrims who traveled to the Holy Land.

Jerusalem, curiously, was not the most well-trodden road, especially in the later Middle Ages. The journey was too long, the cost too high, and the route too dangerous. Far more pilgrims went to holy sites closer to home. Sometimes, however, the least-traveled road is the most precious. Throughout the Middle Ages, Jerusalem still was known as the premier pilgrimage destination. And on maps of the period, this city lay at the center of the known world, reflecting its geographical and spiritual preeminence. Those intrepid pilgrims who were able to make the journey could say they had traveled to the center of all things.

If Jerusalem was the center of the world, the Church of the Holy Sepulchre was the center of Jerusalem. This church, located within the walled Old City, encloses the traditional site of Calvary and the tomb of Christ. Its founding began with a sacred journey. According to legend, Emperor Constantine's mother, Helena, visited Jerusalem in the fourth century. After determining the location of Jesus's tomb, she demolished a pagan temple that had been built on the site and discovered the three crosses of Calvary buried deep beneath it. She discerned which was the cross of Christ, or the "true cross," when it healed a diseased woman. Helena asked Constantine to build a basilica on this sacred site. Completed in 335, the basilica became known as the Church of the Holy Sepulchre. And from that time, the city of Jerusalem drew the world's faithful, who journeyed there to experience the last earthly days of their Lord.

Jerusalem is for travelers from all times and places, including wanderers who will never see its rolling hills or gleaming domes. From early in the Christian tradition, this city has been seen as central to every believer's walk of faith. And in the Middle Ages, the journey there was also a means of instructing the faithful in their spiritual lives. Several medieval mystics and theologians used that frame to teach about a way of life and prayer. Foremost among these teachers was Walter Hilton, a fourteenth-century Augustinian canon. While relatively obscure now, he remains one of the most accessible and down-to-earth mystics of the Middle Ages. As a mystic, Hilton sought to deeply know and experience the presence of God, often through Christian contemplation, silent prayer, and other practices. He numbers among the mystics who have left writings guiding others on the path of drawing near to God.

Hilton hadn't always been a mystic. He first set his sights on becoming a lawyer, studying civil and canon law at Cambridge University. He then began to question this path. He is said to have lived for a time as a hermit before deciding, around 1386, to become an Augustinian Canon Regular, a priest taking vows similar to those of a monk. He remained a canon at Thurgarton Priory in Nottinghamshire until his death in 1396.

Because Hilton had both secular and sacred vocations, he is the ideal guide for contemporary Christians on their journey of faith. He understood that some people are suited to the religious life and others to vocations in the world, yet that all are called to a spiritual life of contemplation and prayer. He was known as a mystic able to help people begin their journey of faith. In the late fourteenth century, as an aid to a woman just beginning her religious life, he wrote a series of instructions, now known as the *Scale of Perfection*. In this book, he responds to the woman's question about what she should do to grow spiritually and to nourish her soul:

> Because you desire a practice to assist the formation of your soul, let me tell you, by the grace of our Lord Jesus, the shortest aid that I know. I will tell you through the example of a good pilgrim.
>
> There was a man wanting to go to Jerusalem, and because he did not know the way he came to another man who he thought could guide him and asked how to reach that city . . . The other man answered and said this: "See, I am setting you on the right road. This is the way, and be sure to keep the instructions I give you."

Those who wish to draw near to Jesus, Hilton continues, should conceive of their life as a pilgrimage. From the physical pilgrims who trod a long and difficult road to the earthly city of Jerusalem, the faithful can learn how to better take their heavenward journey. They receive instruction about its hardships and encouragement to stay on the path of faith. Every Christian, Hilton avows, is a spiritual pilgrim.

Hilton's pilgrim narrative is sometimes called a parable. But in the passage just quoted, Hilton refers to pilgrimage as a "practice." His choice of term is intriguing. We know that physical pilgrimage was an important practice in the Middle Ages. Was spiritual pilgrimage also a practice, a meditative discipline along the lines of contemplative prayer or *lectio divina*, the practice of sacred reading? While Hilton does not offer a manual for spiritual pilgrimage, the lessons and principles he provides are clear, and we will put these in our scrip to aid us on our journey.

Not only was spiritual pilgrimage in the medieval era a reference to a lifelong walk of faith; it also, as I understand it, was an inner path of prayer. Today, people of differing denominations and backgrounds commonly refer to their faith as a spiritual journey. However, we rarely consider prayer itself to be a form of travel. In the thirteenth century, the Franciscan theologian Saint Bonaventure described contemplative, or silent, prayer in just this way. In *The Soul's Journey into God*, he writes of contemplation as a process composed of several stages. At various points, he calls this process a road and a journey that leads to a place of peace. Upon arrival in this place, "the true person of peace rests in the interior Jerusalem." For

Bonaventure and others, prayer is a type of pilgrimage that takes the practitioner deep within, to the place where Jesus awaits.

Whether en route to the physical or the interior Jerusalem, a pilgrim never walks alone. All need guides and companions for the journey.

As we prepare to set out on our Jerusalem road, we find ourselves members of a lively traveling party. Pilgrims like Margery, Felix, and Pietro, along with spiritual mentors like Walter Hilton and Bonaventure, join us on the way. This is very good company. Like the saints and other, better-known figures from history, these pilgrims are members of the great cloud of witnesses of the church eternal.

Yet they are also human. They bring their quirks, their foibles, and their full humanity to the journey. They meet us where we are, with our own foibles and our longing to find a way forward. Each of these pilgrims brings something we need to the journey ahead.

Margery Kempe, an English laywoman and mystic, appeals to the dreamers among us. Passionate about her faith, she makes surprising and sometimes spontaneous decisions in response to it. The written account of her pilgrimage reveals a soul desirous of inner transformation and a traveler who is known for wearing her heart on her sleeve.

Pietro Casola, an Italian canon, brings to the journey his erudition and a delightful sense of humor. His turns of phrase and literary allusions enable us to dig into the deeper realities of what it means to have faith on the pilgrim path.

Felix Fabri, a Swiss Dominican friar, pastors us as we go along. He knows how to dish out a speech, but he also writes with disarming honesty about his many hopes and fears. His vulnerability helps us understand our own. I fell in like with Felix when I observed him address his reader as "beloved brother-wanderer." With my sister-wanderers in mind as well, I have put this phrase in my scrip to use during our travels together.

Each of these wanderers is a mentor for our journey. In their humanity, they help us access our hopes and fears and show us what it means to travel in faith despite the hardships of the road and the challenges we carry within. We will come to know these pilgrims as distinct individuals as we walk with them.

Let's imagine these pilgrims donning their cloak, marked with a cross since they're Jerusalem bound, and strapping on their scrip, into which they've put their coins and a bit of food, along with some extra faith and perseverance. And now we prepare to walk beside them. Accepting their companionship and listening to their stories, we become fellow pilgrims and strangers who are looking for the next country. Together, we'll find inspiration to press on, to take the narrow road, and finally to arrive well at the end.

POINT YOUR feet to JERUSALEM

# 2

# Take the Sure Way

In the early fifteenth century, the English mystic Margery Kempe felt a distinct sense of call to go on pilgrimage. She writes of herself, "Our Lord charged her in her mind, two years before she went, that she go to Rome, to Jerusalem, and to Santiago." Her journey to Jerusalem was the first of these pilgrimages, beginning in the autumn of 1413. After that, she made a lengthy stopover in Rome and then, two years later, a trip to Santiago de Compostela.

Margery's spiritual tour began with the biggest journey of all, the epic voyage to Jerusalem. If we look at a medieval map of the world—the Hereford Mappa Mundi, for example—we see the challenge that awaited her. On this and other maps of the period, Jerusalem lies at the center of the circular world; England (where the map was created) hugs the edge. An English pilgrim like Margery thus traveled half the known world to arrive at Jerusalem, this most sacred of sites.

In our own travels, we often plot the most direct route possible, but Margery and other pilgrims zigged and zagged across long distances to reach their destination. They experienced all kinds of detours, connections, layovers, and delays. Their journeys seem remarkably inefficient and often led through terrain we'd think twice about braving. Pilgrims' routes are worth following because they tell us a good deal about the motivations of the seekers who embarked on these monumental journeys—and the faith that was required to carry them through.

Preparing for a lengthy trip today, many of us find it helpful to have a printed itinerary. If we plugged the typical journey of a late medieval pilgrim into a contemporary format, it might look something like the itinerary shown here.

# TRAVEL ITINERARY

## *Leg 1*
**Depart from: Home        To: Venice**
**By: Foot, Horse, Mule**

Departure Time: Late winter/early spring
Duration: 2 weeks–2 months

## *Leg 2*
**Layover in Venice**

Duration: 4 weeks–3 months
Lodging: Inn
Activities: Sightsee; change currency; book
travel to the Holy Land

## *Leg 3*
**Depart from: Venice        To: Jaffa**
**By: Sailing galley**

Departure Time: Spring/summer
Duration: 5–6 weeks
Shipboard activities: Avoid illness; pray; survive

*Leg 4*
**Layover in Jaffa**

Duration: 5–14 days
Lodging: Underground cellars or galley
Activities: Avoid illness; scrounge for food;
go through customs

*Leg 5*
**Depart from: Jaffa        To: Jerusalem**
**By: Donkey**

Departure Time: Whim of local officials
Duration of trip: 3 days
Layovers: City of Ramla; campsite in Judea

This basic itinerary—from home to Venice to Jaffa to Jerusalem—remained the fairly fixed route for European travelers in the later Middle Ages. Individual journeys would, of course, vary. And because everyone had a different starting point, especially in the first leg, no two pilgrimages looked alike. An important principle of pilgrimage, one often forgotten today, is its beginning: the journey is launched the moment a pilgrim walks out her front door.

On our own journeys, we usually think of traveling *to* a starting point and *then* beginning our visit or pilgrimage. Americans wanting to walk the Camino de Santiago, for example, fly to France or Spain and "begin" their journey from there. The walking portion—and thus the real pilgrimage, it is assumed—starts at one of the cities along the historical route. This tourist mind-set is related to mechanized modes of travel. But medievals knew that a true pilgrimage always begins the moment you leave your house.

Understanding this principle helps us see that there are as many routes as there are dwelling places, as many unique paths as there are people striking out in the name of faith. In the Middle Ages, pilgrims to Jerusalem began their path from villages and hamlets throughout Europe. On the map at the beginning of this book, we can follow the routes of our three pilgrim mentors as they made their way to the Holy Land. Let's look for a moment at the first leg of their journey. Margery Kempe set off from her hometown of Bishop's Lynn, in Norfolk, England, and traveled through the Holy Roman Empire to the city of Konstanz, in southern Germany. A few years later, Felix Fabri departed from his convent at Ulm, in Swabia, a historic region in southwestern Germany. His path took him to the Alpine city of Innsbruck. Margery and Felix then crossed the Alps and made their way to Venice.

The first part of Pietro Casola's journey took place exclusively in Italy. He began in Milan and traveled through the cities of Verona, Vicenza, and Padua. A good many non-European pilgrims traveled to Jerusalem, too. Some journeyed to the Holy Land from the Christian kingdoms of Africa. One such route that may have been taken by the Nubian king Moses George has been traced on the map.

Sooner or later, the paths of most European pilgrims led to Venice. From this point, their routes had more in common. Pilgrims left Venice in a ship, sailing across the Mediterranean Sea to Jaffa, a port city in historic Palestine, and rode donkeys inland to Jerusalem. And once they arrived in the sacred city itself, pilgrims followed a set itinerary as local guides took them to various sites.

The timing of the voyage was a bit more up in the air but just as essential as the route. To avoid winter storms, galleys sailed from Venice in spring or summer. The entire pilgrimage hinged on the departure date of these ships, which was neither set in stone nor well advertised. Preparing for his journey in the spring of 1494, Pietro informed himself, through Venetian friends, of the departure window of the galleys. If he were to miss the boat, he might have to wait from several months to a year for the next departure.

Given the vagaries of travel and the uncertainty of the timing, it's almost surprising so many pilgrims made it to Jerusalem. And it's more than a little surprising that, knowing the risks, they still set out for the center of the world.

In the chapters that follow, we'll journey with pilgrims along the route in the sample itinerary. At each leg, we will pause, take in the view, observe the conditions these pilgrims endured, and then see what we can learn about our own walk of faith.

Yes, each journey begins as we go out the door, but let's begin *this* journey by considering the end. For the first lesson of our pilgrimage is this: before we even walk out our front door, we need to know where to point our feet. Our three mentors—Margery, Felix, and Pietro—set off from places in England and Europe, but they all ended up in Jerusalem. How I relish the image of these individual paths converging upon, flowing into, and meeting up in the city at the center of the world.

It perhaps goes without saying that this trajectory holds for you and me as well. On the journey of faith, our destination is Jerusalem. Along with all of God's people from all times and places, we are on our way to the glorious city God has prepared for us. We read about it in the book of Hebrews, which describes the great cloud of witnesses who accompany us on this journey. In Hebrews 11, the writer rehearses the merits of such figures as Abel, Noah, Abraham, and Sarah and defines their faith as a journey to a longed-for destination:

> All these people were still living by faith when they died. They did not receive the things promised; they only saw them and welcomed them from a distance, admitting that they were foreigners and strangers on earth. People who say such things show that they are looking for a country of their own. If they had been thinking of the country they had left, they would have had opportunity to return. Instead, they were longing for a better country—a heavenly one. Therefore God is not ashamed to be called their God, for he has prepared a city for them. (Hebrews 11:13–16 NIV)

The heavenly Jerusalem beckons the faithful. It called Abraham and his kin, and it calls out to us. Traveling there, we are part of Hebrews' great cloud, which I like to imagine as a brilliantly colored sky flowing toward an unseen horizon.

In the Middle Ages, theologians and other writers responded to the primacy of Jerusalem perhaps more than we do today. Over and over, this city is identified as the goal of a pilgrim's spiritual journey. As Walter Hilton wrote about the "good pilgrim" setting his face toward Jerusalem, he encourages us to do the same. All who go in this direction, Hilton says, take the "sure way." It is important that Hilton's pilgrim doesn't travel just anywhere—not to Santiago de Compostela, or Canterbury, or the shrine in the neighboring village. Only Jerusalem represents the sure way. This is the road that leads to Jesus. It's the road that takes us home.

Focusing on our destination sounds distinctly countercultural today. Often, when it comes to pilgrimage, we hear sayings like "It's the journey that matters" or "The search is the meaning." Yet this viewpoint would have been unimaginable for medieval pilgrims. Sometimes we forget that, historically, a pilgrimage almost always had an endpoint. The pilgrim arrived! The goal was attained! The journey was completed! Yes, the act of travel might itself have been transformational, but it led pilgrims to a single destination the way a well-shot arrow hits its mark.

For pilgrims like Margery Kempe, Felix Fabri, and Pietro Casola, the destination mattered. Adventures along the road did teach them important lessons, such as patience, perseverance, and an understanding of suffering. Yet these pilgrims always kept Jerusalem, kept Jesus, in their sights. And knowing their goal, they kept going.

We moderns tend to resist the idea of a destination, says author James K. A. Smith, because we love freedom, even though we often misunderstand what it means. Being free, we think, means hitting the road with the wind whipping our hair and no one telling us where or when or even *that* we have to be somewhere. So we make the road into our dwelling place. We mistake it for the better country that lies ahead.

The irony, Smith suggests, "is that we experience frustration and disappointment when we try to make the road a home rather than realizing it's *leading* us home, when we try to tell ourselves 'the road is life.'" True freedom lies in walking a road that has already been blazed, in following a way we don't have to make ourselves, because someone has thoughtfully paved (or at least weeded) it for us. And it lies in knowing that that *someone* is waiting at the end with a light and a meal and rest for our weary feet.

The road tempts us to think we can go our own way and create our own destiny. But "never arriving means you're always leaving," writes Smith. It means you never come home.

Throughout Scripture, the home to which we journey goes by many names: a place of peace; a city on a hill; a house of many rooms; the New Jerusalem. We may not be able to clearly picture or fathom this home that awaits us, but we know what it represents. We can *feel* its promises even if we cannot see them. Home promises the beginning of our new, fully transformed selves. When we come home, Jesus will complete the good work begun in us. When we come home, "every kind of thing will be well," as Dame Julian of Norwich writes.

Lessons do, of course, happen along our slow journey home. Our pilgrimage path is where life is lived; it is where we love, grow, make mistakes, and learn. Sometimes the lessons and mistakes knock us down rather more than we'd like. But for the one who pilgrims to Jerusalem for the love of God, there is good news: we know where the path leads. So much in life remains uncertain, but our destination does not. All our steps, and even our missteps, lead to our forever home with Jesus.

When I think on my own journey, I realize how much I crave this assurance. The last few years of my life have brought so many surprises that I've grown wary of the next bend in the road. I catch myself peering ahead with reluctance and anxiety. But I'm learning to take the long view, one that looks past the next curve to a destination that increasingly seems like the only sure thing along life's path.

I still might find that a future bend in the road harbors an unpleasant surprise or a circumstance beyond my control. But looking ahead—much farther into the distance—provides some correction to spiritual myopia. It is simply untenable to go through life in a bewildered haze, afraid to see what lies before us. Like our three pilgrims, we can learn to direct our gaze to what is good and true. To long for it and to sigh for it, as Saint Augustine says, and then to walk toward it, step by slow and steady step.

Now, we don't know everything about this distant home that captures our gaze. A paradox of pilgrimage, the first of many we'll explore, is that we are journeying toward a home we have not seen. We usually think of home as a place we remember, a safe space for which we long after a time away. I think, for example, of the ancestral home to which I traveled on my Great American Pilgrimage a few holidays ago. When it comes to pilgrimage, however, "joy is arriving at the home you've never been to," writes Smith. We long for a place that is completely foreign yet that resonates with a note we're sure we have heard before. So as we go along, we wonder. We hope. We journey in faith, believing that when we finally arrive, we will experience the frisson of déjà vu. Our home will be the familiar place we never knew.

Having a destination doesn't lessen the import of the journey itself. It does not curb our freedom or negate our very real need for sustenance and joy in the here and now. Rather, our destination allows us to live life to the full because we can let go of the great worry many of us have: Where is my life going?

The pilgrim Margery Kempe arrived at her destination in the spring of 1414. Upon catching her first glimpse of Jerusalem, she requested and received a special gift. Looking upon the earthly city, she asked Jesus to grant her a vision of the heavenly Jerusalem above. The vision she received so moved her with joy that two companions had to keep her from falling off her donkey.

I sometimes wonder what it will be like when, at the end of the road, we see our destination opening before us, as it did for medieval pilgrims seeing the first glimmer of Jerusalem's domes. The city will surely be host to the greatest reunion ever known, since it serves as the common destination for every traveler on the road of Christian faith—Margery, Felix, Pietro, all of us. Our unique paths, each one stamped with the course God has set for it, will one day converge upon the city at the center of the world. This makes me glad, for it means we will see each other there. We will arrive to worship in Jerusalem together.

So as we face ourselves in the right direction, we aim to take our first step. We're ready to embark on the sure way. Wherever we are—in a good place, in a bad place, in no particular or special place—we point our feet in the direction of Jerusalem.

: TAKE THE SURE WAY

# 3

# Write Your Will

Pilgrims' travel guides offered all manner of advice for those wanting to point their feet to Jerusalem. Many are a mix of the practical and spiritual. One guide, published in 1481 by Cavalier Santo Brasca, a prominent diplomat from Milan, gives a series of instructions that include, first and foremost, going for the right reason: "In the first place, a pilgrim should undertake this voyage solely with the intention of visiting, contemplating and adoring the most Holy Mysteries, and not with the intention of seeing the world, or from ambition, or to be able to boast 'I have been there,' or 'I have seen that.' The pilgrim who boasts receives nothing but an earthly reward." Only after imparting this bit of advice does Santo talk of more practical preparations, such as procuring a long overcoat and a supply of good Lombard cheese.

Santo continues, "Secondly, the pilgrim should put his affairs in order and make a will, so that whatever God wills to happen, his heirs may not find themselves in difficulties." When Santo refers to "whatever God wills to happen," it's his gentle way of saying, "in case the pilgrim dies." For Santo, preparing for death was second in importance only to preparing the right attitude.

For pilgrims today, this sobering advice gives pause. It seems surprising to hear the risks of the journey so bluntly stated. Yet such a warning was necessary, for the medieval road to Jerusalem invited danger and uncertainty. It involved a long journey over mountains and across the sea, often in times of war, and led straight into territory held in the late Middle Ages by Mamluk sultans, who had a contentious relationship with visitors from the West. Beyond that, the greatest threat to pilgrims came from illness and disease, which spread rapidly on crowded sailing galleys and in foreign lands.

When Pietro Casola wrote an account of his 1494 journey to Jerusalem, he punctuated his narrative at disturbingly regular intervals with the untimely

deaths of pilgrims in his party. Especially dishearten-
ing are the accounts of those who did not live long
enough to even glimpse Jerusalem. On July 31, during the pilgrims' sea crossing, Pietro tersely notes,
"One of the pilgrims—a Frenchman—died, and was
buried on the seashore. This was the third pilgrim
who died before we could go to Jerusalem."

An even direr situation befell some pilgrims setting off from Africa in the thirteenth century. Moses
George, a king of Nubia, told a tragic tale to a group
of French knights and barons he met in the Holy
Land: of the sixty companions with whom he set out,
only ten had made it all the way to Jerusalem. African
pilgrims followed a different path than those beginning in Europe but met with equal risk. The possible
route of Moses George can be seen on the map in this
book. Desert crossings, coupled with political unrest
in Egypt and Palestine, were so dangerous for African
pilgrims that one Ethiopian king established a local
site, a "Holy Land in Ethiopia," so that pilgrims could
make a safer holy quest.

Given the risks of long-distance pilgrimage, the
settling of affairs topped the list of tasks for would-
be travelers. These tasks included getting permission
to depart, usually from a bishop or overlord. Pilgrimage to Jerusalem required papal license. When Margery Kempe prepared to travel to Jerusalem, she also

secured permission from her husband, which was necessary for a woman undertaking such a journey. She then settled both their debts. "She asked the parish priest of the town where she was living to say in the pulpit for her that, if any man or woman claimed any debt of her husband or her, they should come and speak with her before she went; and she, with God's help, would settle the debt with each of them so they could consider themselves content."

Margery's decision to go to Jerusalem was far from spontaneous. The trip took two years of planning and preparation. We don't know, however, what preparations she made for the care of her fourteen children during her absence. For many today, Margery's willingness to leave her family behind makes her a controversial figure in the history of pilgrimage. She reminds us that we all come to the journey with unique life situations—with families, desires, problems, and what sometimes seem to onlookers like dubious decisions.

The call to pilgrimage overtook everything else in Margery's life. In her account, she writes of her great desire to see the places where the Lord had lived, suffered, and died. Her choice, whatever we think of it, prompts us to consider how the demands and urgency of the spiritual journey might interrupt our life—and what would be our response if they do.

In the Middle Ages, a journey to Jerusalem would have involved a consideration of costs for every person, not just Margery Kempe. To take this trip, men and women alike left their families, jobs, lands, and responsibilities. Potential pilgrims had to ask themselves, *What am I able to leave behind? What risks are acceptable for me to take?* No long-distance pilgrimage, as we saw from Santo Brasca's advice, came with a guarantee of return. That is why many pilgrims, after getting their finances and permissions in order, also wrote a will. Before leaving for Jerusalem in 1419, the Frenchman Nompar, Lord of Caumont, drafted a lengthy testament in which he made provisions for his time away. He entrusted his family and lands to temporary governors and solicited daily masses. He then turned his attention to more delicate matters. In the event that God "had his pleasure with him" while he was in the Holy Land, he named his oldest son the heir of his properties and title. He also entreated those who would be left behind to devotedly pray for God's mercy and for the resurrection of his body.

This pilgrim was prepared, at least on paper, to travel not only to the Kingdom of Jerusalem but also to the heavenly kingdom. His departure from home ushered him into a liminal state in which he was neither fully alive nor fully dead. The murky status of pilgrims explains the tearful leave-takings that marked the beginning of many of their journeys. "To other humans those on pilgrimage were conventionally and legally considered to be dying," notes scholar Celia Lewis.

It must have been difficult for pilgrims themselves to fully live into this liminal status. For many, it appears to have heightened their lust for life, which is on full display in travel accounts. Those who went on pilgrimage packed their favorite foods and pursued whatever small comforts they could find. They also relished new experiences, such as sightseeing in Venice while awaiting their sea passage. They visited churches and monasteries but also appreciated the cultural splendor of Venice, with its ceremonies, harbors, and markets. Pietro describes the wines made in each port of call on his journey and seems impressed by the variety available in the Venetian markets. These wines are very good, this proud Milanese notes, "although they are not so perfect as ours."

Although some pleasures were to be had on the journey to Jerusalem, the well-advertised risks sobered pilgrims enough for them to prepare for their possible demise. But clearly they did not want to be declared dead *too* soon. In his testament, Nompar of Caumont advised that, whatever rumors his family and lieges might hear, they should not presume him dead before receiving sufficient proof or before one year had passed.

Similar time stipulations were made concerning the remaining spouse's remarriage. In a thirteenth-century miracle story by Caesarius of Heisterbach, a Cistercian monk, we read about a knight preparing for a lengthy pilgrimage. The knight "broke a gold ring into two pieces before the eyes of his wife, and joining them together in her presence, gave one piece to her and kept the other himself, saying, 'You ought to trust this token. Moreover, I ask you to wait five years for my return, and after that you can marry any one you please.'" In the story, time passes. A lot of time. All seems lost. At the last possible moment, the pilgrim returns to claim his wife, only to find her celebrating her wedding feast with another man. Although fictional, Caesarius's tale provides a glimpse into a common medieval practice. The dangers of long-distance pilgrimage, coupled with a lack of reliable communication, made this rather grim preparation necessary.

Perhaps more than any other plans made by medieval pilgrims, the preparation for a spouse's remarriage snags at my heart. When I put myself in a pilgrim's place, imagining my permanent absence is a little too concrete for comfort. Many of us walk this path of imagination when we write our will, but our considerations are probably related to financial security rather than a spouse's future companion.

This practice of settling debt and writing a will—and indeed the whole enterprise of pilgrimage—flies in the face of our risk-averse culture. If we felt called to make a pilgrimage or another journey that came with little probability of our safe return, would we go? The litmus test for me is whether I would let my children go. The answer, usually, is no. But what if God wanted us to take some such risk in our physical or spiritual life? The truth is that we are so addicted to comfort and safety that it can be nearly impossible to live boldly. As a friend of mine says, "We have become curators of caution rather than harbingers of hope."

In pilgrimage accounts and in the stories of Scripture, nowhere are there promises of a safe ride through life. Instead, Jesus offers a sobering statement counseling his followers to be prepared to leave everything behind: "For whoever wants to save their life will lose it, but whoever loses their life for me will find it" (Matthew 16:25 NIV). This challenging verse reminds us of the risks of our journey and also its hope. The road to Jerusalem is an invitation to jump off the edge of the known and trust that Jesus will be there when we do.

Walter Hilton may have had such challenges in mind when he wrote *The Scale of Perfection*. As he explains the practice of spiritual pilgrimage, he introduces the parable of a man planning to go to Jerusalem. In this parable, the man does not set out immediately; he must first prepare his heart and mind. From a guide, the man learns of the dangers he's likely to face: he will travel a long and difficult way; he will encounter enemies; he will be robbed and beaten. The would-be pilgrim must then decide whether or not to set out.

Just as Hilton's pilgrim faces an eventful journey, so do all who embark on the spiritual road. As pilgrims of faith, we should become aware of the risks involved before making our decision. Knowing that the journey will cause us distress, are we willing to travel? Will we follow Jesus to Jerusalem?

It's a journey that will cost us dearly. When Jesus made his own way to Jerusalem, he told the crowds a parable about preparing for discipleship: "Suppose one of you wants to build a tower. Won't you first sit down and estimate the cost to see if you have enough money to complete it? For if you lay the foundation and are not able to finish it, everyone who sees it will ridicule you, saying, 'This person began to build and wasn't able to finish'" (Luke 14:28–30 NIV).

In case anyone in the crowd wondered what this cost might be, Jesus immediately launched into another parable leaving little doubt. Relating the story of a king weighing his resources in times of war, Jesus concluded, "In the same way, those of you who do not give up everything you have cannot be my disciples" (Luke 14:33 NIV). Given that Jesus uttered this on his way to the cross—his own renunciation—the message takes on a profound resonance and highlights the cost.

When Jesus said that a person must "give up everything," he truly meant *every thing*. For those of us on a spiritual pilgrimage, there is nothing we can hold onto; and that includes our very life. In an interview about the Gospel of Mark, Eugene Peterson said, "The first half of the Gospel is Jesus showing people how to live. He's healing everybody. Then right in the middle, he shifts. He starts showing people how to die: 'Now that you've got a life, I'm going to show you how to give it up.' That's the whole spiritual life. It's learning how to die."

I'm heartened that Peterson used the word *learning*, for giving up your life doesn't happen all at once.

I know that it certainly doesn't for me. I cling to what I erroneously call life, like a miser clutching her sacks of coins. In one sack is the control I want to exercise over every detail of my life; in another is my sense of entitlement that tells me I am owed an easier time. Many other sacks hold the misplaced desires that lead me off my chosen path. How difficult it is to die to these parts of myself. They are prized possessions that I hoard. But as I take the first steps of my journey, I am learning what it means to cast them off.

As I take these steps, I look to our pilgrim mentors for courage. Reading about Margery Kempe's settling of debts and Nompar of Caumont's call to draw up a will, I gaze upon my life and consider the cost. Am I ready to leave behind my comforts and my entitlement—those twin barriers to a life of faith? Can I go forward without them? These questions led me to develop a spiritual exercise to help myself and others prepare for the journey ahead. When I lead retreats, I assign an exercise entitled Spiritual Will Writing 101. Together, retreatants and I acknowledge that we are pilgrims on the road to Jerusalem. As such, we prepare to leave our life behind. We write a will in which we bequeath our misplaced wants and desires to Jesus. Detailing these desires—the ones that focus on our own comfort at all costs—helps us see to what extent they have become treasures to which we cling. We then ask Jesus to give us the strength to leave them behind. This exercise is as much for my benefit as for that of retreat participants. It is good practice in dying.

In those retreats we also remember, with prayer, the pilgrims who physically died on their journey to the Holy Land. Some pilgrims even wished to die. Earlier we met King Moses George of Nubia, who left Africa on a pilgrimage to Jerusalem in the early thirteenth century. Although most of his companions perished along the way, Moses George planned to pursue his travels to the end of the road. A chronicler who spoke to the Nubian king in Constantinople reports, "And he said that he wanted to go on pilgrimage to Rome and from Rome to Santiago de Compostela, and then come back to Jerusalem, if he should live so long, and then die there." This pilgrim could think of no better end to his travels than ascending to Jesus in the holy city.

This wish of Moses George reminds me of the reason I make my own pilgrimage. As the Cavalier Brasca cautioned, it's not to boast in my progress. Nor is it to travel so cautiously that I seek at all costs to preserve my life. It is, rather, to come ever closer to the embrace of Jesus.

Despite the reminder, I am often filled with regret at my decision to travel this road that requires me to learn how to die. I miss those twin sacks of comfort and control I am called to renounce, and I chafe at the writing of my spiritual will. Yet every day, I rehearse like a mantra, "I am pointing my feet in the right direction. I am taking the sure way." And I cling to this hope, this certainty. I invite you to hope with me. The spiritual path requires much of us. Some days we might struggle to leave our baggage behind, and on those days, it can be enough simply to rehearse this mantra. To reclaim our pilgrim identity. And to gather our courage to take a single step forward.

Journey

I AM NOTHING;
I HAVE NOTHING;
I DESIRE NOTHING
BUT THE
LOVE OF JESUS
...ALONE.

FELIX FABRI

# 4

## Stay the Course

In the spring of 1480, Friar Felix Fabri left his hometown of Ulm, in southwestern Germany, and set his face toward Jerusalem. He undertook several preparations before leaving. He fretted about money, and he jetted to and fro, asking advice about the journey. When Felix asked Count Eberhard the Elder, a nobleman of Wurtemburg, if he should truly commit to the pilgrimage, the count gave this tongue-in-cheek response:

> There are three acts in a person's life which no one ought to advise them to do or not to do. The first is to contract matrimony, the second is to go to war, the third is to visit the Holy Sepulchre

in Jerusalem. These three acts are good in themselves, but they may easily turn out ill; and when
this is so, the one who gave the advice comes to
be blamed as if he were the cause of its turning
out ill.

Still, in the end, Count Eberhard went against his
own maxim and advised Felix to go to Jerusalem as
long as his motives were pure.

Felix's pilgrimage did not turn out ill, but it had
a rough beginning, as some journeys do. On Sunday,
April 9, Felix stood before his congregation in Ulm
and preached a sermon in which he announced his
intention to depart for Jerusalem. Fearing for his life,
many congregants sobbed through the singing of the
daily hymns. Five days later, Felix received the pilgrim's blessing, mounted his horse, and made the
short ride to Memmingen, where he took an emotional leave of his spiritual mentor, Master Ludwig,
the prior of the convent at Ulm. At this point, the pilgrimage nearly ended before it had even begun. "After
my spiritual father's departure," Felix wrote,

> a great and almost irresistible temptation
> assailed me, for the delightful eagerness to see
> Jerusalem and the holy places, with which I had
> until that time been glowing, altogether died
> within me, and I felt a loathing for travel; and the

pilgrimage, which had appeared so sweet and virtuous, now seemed wearisome, bitter, useless, empty, and sinful. I was angry with myself for having undertaken it, and all those who had dissuaded me from it I now thought to be the wisest of counselors and the truest of friends; while I considered that those who had encouraged me were enemies of my life. I had more pleasure in beholding Swabia than the land of Canaan, and Ulm appeared to me pleasanter than Jerusalem. Moreover, the fear of the sea increased within me, and I conceived so many objections to that pilgrimage that, had I not been ashamed, I would have run after Master Ludwig and re-entered Ulm with him, and I should have had the greatest delight in doing so.

The temptation to turn back plagued Felix throughout his pilgrimage.

When I first read the overwrought language of this lament, I smiled. But once I got past its rhetorical flourishes, it endeared me to Felix. I sensed authenticity beneath the embellishment. That such a resourceful traveler would feel the urge to turn back speaks across the centuries to those of us for whom the call to adventure comes with a healthy dose of trepidation.

Felix's hesitation is understandable, given an impending journey of close to three thousand miles.

His trek would take him over the Alps, across the Mediterranean Sea, and into a foreign land. He walked, rode mules, and sailed through war-torn waters.

We can follow Felix's journey on a map, such as the one at the beginning of this book. But we cannot replicate his mode of travel, which is very much of its time. There are still a few intrepid people who go by foot from Europe to Jerusalem, but most who want to "go medieval" do so by walking the Camino de Santiago, a network of routes that wind through Europe to the Cathedral of Santiago de Compostela in Spain. Parts of this network are rigorous. The Camino Francés route, for example, crosses the French Pyrenees and is known for its unpredictable weather. As Felix did on his journey, pilgrims who walk the Camino Francés or other paths often express an urge to stop. In a recent account of her pilgrimage on the Camino, author Phileena Heuertz writes that she often hit a wall, a limit beyond which it seemed she could not go. "My body, mind and emotions all reached their limit at virtually the same time. Every muscle, bone, joint and tendon seemed to be shouting for me to stop," Heuertz confesses.

The hardships of pilgrimage often have a mental element, too, as physical struggles merge with emotional exhaustion or homesickness. Not just pilgrimage, but any kind of travel can lead to a longing for the home we've left behind. Sometimes we set off on the path, and even though we've already paid for the journey and booked our hotel, we immediately regret our decision. The path we've chosen may be the right one, but we just want to be at home with our books and our cats and our favorite coffee mug.

Our medieval traveler, Friar Felix, invokes a popular biblical story to explain how his own home-sickness became a full-blown crisis of faith. In the passage about his temptation to turn back, he writes, "I had more pleasure in beholding Swabia than the land of Canaan, and Ulm appeared to me pleasanter than Jerusalem." Recall that the city of Ulm, in Swabia, is Felix's hometown. In this passage, Felix is contrasting his yearning for home with his previously expressed desire for Jerusalem. He likens Jerusalem to "Canaan," which evokes the Israelites' journey to the Promised Land. In the Hebrew Bible, the book of Exodus describes how, when Moses led the Israelites out of captivity and in the direction of Canaan, they grumbled at the difficulties of the journey and longed for the land of their oppressors. "Wouldn't it be better for us to go back to Egypt?" they said to Moses (Numbers 14:3 NIV).

Similarly, Felix struggles with a desire to remain in his own personal Egypt, even though his travels would take him to the land he professed such a desire to see. He does not want God to take him on a journey requiring that he leave everything familiar about his surroundings, his life, and possibly his innermost self.

With a pastor's heart, Felix touches on a dilemma that defines not just his own journey, but that of all followers of Jesus. Jesus calls us to the Promised Land—a land Jesus has set apart for us, a land flowing with milk and honey. Moreover, Jesus promises to be our guide the entire way. But when it comes down to it, many of us simply don't want to go. Resistance, fear, and habit hold us back. In his book *Leaving Egypt*, author Chuck DeGroat reflects on the nature of spiritual journeys, concluding, with great honesty, that his own heart is "relentlessly committed to its many Egypts." It's a common problem, he says. Old habits and ingrained ways of thinking tempt us to believe we are better off where we are (or were), even though Jesus beckons us to a better place.

History's mystics and theologians understand the problem of Egypt. In *The Scale of Perfection*, our medieval guide Walter Hilton writes that one of the biggest dangers of our spiritual pilgrimage is the temptation to give up or turn back. In his book, he personifies this temptation as a group of enemies who badger us as we try to move forward. Fear is one such enemy. Another is carnal desire, which speaks to our inclination to embrace comfort rather than challenge. When I become aware of a deficiency in my spiritual life or sense that all is not right with my heart, I often will attempt to fill the gap with food, TV, sex, or sleep rather than taking the difficult steps toward growth.

Hilton's description of temptation as a group of menacing thugs resonates with me. He personifies these temptations so that we will grasp their danger. There is nothing abstract about them; they are true enemies of our journey. Sidling up to us, these enemies begin with flattery. *Maybe no one else sees how hard you've been working, but we do. You deserve to take it easier.* Seeing us waver, they grow bolder, trying to convince us that the way is just too difficult. Finally, our foes pronounce, "And therefore turn home again and leave this desire, for you will never carry it through to the end."

The twentieth-century mystic and theologian Howard Thurman notes that not just enemies, but also the demands of daily life, can wreak havoc on our journey. In one of his meditations, he describes a weakening of the "high resolve" with which he began his own spiritual path:

> There was no intent to betray what seemed so sure at the time. My response was whole, clean, authentic. But little by little, there crept into my life the dust and grit of the journey. Details, lower-level demands, all kinds of crosscurrents—nothing momentous, nothing overwhelming, nothing flagrant—just wear and tear. If there had been some direct challenge—a clear-cut issue—I would have fought it to the end, and beyond.

Thurman writes that he asked God to "keep fresh before me the moments of my High Resolve, that . . . I may not forget that to which my life is committed."

Walter Hilton and Howard Thurman help us to see why all spiritual pilgrims from time to time feel tempted to turn back. Enemies and daily wear and tear sound the siren call of Egypt. There is no shame in hearing this call. Our pilgrim mentor Felix Fabri heard it, and so will we. Our resolve, like Felix's, might weaken. Sometimes, we may even have to step away from the path for a bit. Our backpack becomes so heavy that we must set it down.

Such pauses are a normal part of the pilgrimage process, says spiritual writer Christine Valters Paintner. Setting down our backpack does not mean that we're failing or that we've lost our faith, she assures us. It simply means that we're human. "The problem is not with the waning of our inner fire and perseverance," she writes. "We are human beings and go through times of dryness." But we don't pause forever. Paintner continues: "What becomes soul killing is not returning at all . . . We need practices to act as touchstones so they can sustain us during our journey."

A key practice, Paintner finds, involves "beginning again." We should expect to falter and be willing to rejoin the path as many times as it takes. This practice is rooted in the wisdom of Saint Benedict of Nursia, often called the "father of Western monasticism." Benedict called his rule for monasteries a "little rule for beginners." I appreciate the gentleness of this practice. Sometimes it is just what I need, especially when I try to convince myself that I shouldn't need periods of rest or resetting. At these times, I remember that I may (temporarily) leave the path, but the path is still there, waiting for me. I can always begin again.

Sometimes, though, I need a bit more prodding. I need the fire of Howard Thurman's meditation or Walter Hilton's *Scale of Perfection*, which offer bold advice for persevering on the pilgrimage road. Thurman suggests that we pray for resolve, while Hilton tells us to talk back to our spiritual enemies. Let's explore in more detail what Hilton means by this unusual piece of advice. When we are tempted to turn away from our path, Hilton writes, we should first say to ourselves, "I want to be in Jerusalem." Recalling our goal, we refuse to be distracted or to give in to fear-mongering. If our enemies persist in their badgering, we should speak directly to them. We turn up the volume and confront them with these words: "I am nothing; I have nothing; I desire nothing but the love of Jesus alone."

This phrase, Hilton writes, puts humility and love in our heart. "Humility says, I am nothing; I have nothing. Love says, I desire only one thing, and that is Jesus." This humility is not a devaluation of ourselves, but a way to inspire greater confidence in Jesus. Taken together, Hilton's words give us courage by reminding us—and our enemies—why we are making our pilgrimage. We want to be in Jerusalem.

In his book, Hilton repeats this phrase three times, with slight variations. For those on a spiritual pilgrimage, it's his number-one piece of advice for staying the course. The meditative nature of Hilton's phrase, coupled with its repetition, has the quality of a mantra—a short, repeated saying meant to boost concentration or awareness. While mantras are often associated with Eastern religions, the Christian contemplative tradition has short sayings and prayers that are intended for a similar purpose.

Christian contemplation includes a variety of practices: *lectio divina*, or sacred reading; imaginative gospel meditation, in the vein of Ignatius of Loyola's *Spiritual Exercises*; and resting in silence with God. This third practice is often called contemplative or centering prayer. Centering prayer typically uses a single word, which Trappist monk and priest Basil Pennington calls a love word, to be repeated or held in awareness as a person sits silently with God. The author of *The Cloud of Unknowing*, a fourteenth-century contemplative guide, advises choosing a very simple word, such as *God*. One could also use *Jesus* or *maranatha*. Pennington writes, "I know a very beautiful sister for whom the prayer word is 'let go.'" The point is not the word itself, but the way in which it announces our intention to be present to God or helps us return to God when our attention wanders.

Another prayer mantra is the Jesus Prayer: "Lord Jesus Christ, Son of God, have mercy on me." This mantra originated in the early centuries of Eastern Christianity and also forms the central prayer of the nineteenth-century book *The Way of a Pilgrim*. It is meant to be recited at intervals and then as a matter of habit. Through this practice, the Jesus Prayer becomes rooted in a pilgrim's heart and mind, helping her to pray continually and remain focused on the inner path.

Alongside the love word and the Jesus Prayer, Walter Hilton's affirmation is a short burst of encouragement we can put in our scrip and repeat on our pilgrimage. "I am nothing; I have nothing; I desire nothing but the love of Jesus alone."

Once, when leading a retreat, I asked participants to repeat this mantra as they walked the labyrinth on the retreat grounds. We found that it helped focus the mind while following the slow and winding course to our "Jerusalem" at the center of the path. If you enjoy labyrinths or meditative walks, Hilton's mantra can be an effective aid for these journeys.

I also pause and recite Hilton's mantra when the going gets rough during the course of a regular day. It slows me down. It quiets my mind. It reminds me that I am a pilgrim on my way to Jerusalem. You, my fellow travelers, might find it useful, too. Say Hilton's mantra to remind yourself where you're going and why. Say it often, because you will need it often. "I am nothing; I have nothing; I desire nothing but the love of Jesus alone." These words will not take away the hardships of your journey. They will not prevent you from yearning to turn back. But they might give you courage to stay the course. They will remind you that you can attain your heart's desire.

For all his fears, his setbacks, and his temptation to abandon the path, Friar Felix the pilgrim attained his fondest desire. He remained on the road and reached the sacred city of Jerusalem. Not only did Felix stay the course, he returned on pilgrimage to the Holy Land a second time!

Beloved brother- and sister-wanderers, taking our cue from Felix, let us stay on the road.

We *will* reach Jerusalem.

ALPS

EACH PILGRIM HAS
NEED OF THREE SACKS:
A SACK OF PATIENCE,
A SACK OF MONEY,
AND A SACK OF FAITH.

**5**

# Cross the Alps

In the later Middle Ages, every Jerusalem pilgrim came face-to-face with a wall of ice and rock. Pilgrims settled their affairs, left their homes, stayed the course, and walked until they hit the Alps. This chain of mountains, some seven hundred miles long, stood directly in their path. No autobahns or tunnels helped them pass; if pilgrims wanted to reach Jerusalem, they had to cross these mountains on foot. As pilgrims looked up at the snowy peaks, the monumental scale of their journey must have sunk in, perhaps for the first time. The real challenges, both physical and spiritual, were about to begin.

For all but the most adventurous among us, plotting a route that crosses four thousand vertical feet of rock and snow sounds absurd. It flies in the face of our culture of convenience, which tells us to always take the easiest and most direct route. In this light, an Alpine crossing of such magnitude makes the pilgrimage journey look foolish. Was there no other way to get to Jerusalem?

Sometimes, there was. In earlier centuries, many pilgrims to the Holy Land avoided the Alps entirely. Their routes varied, but they tended to follow Roman roads, traveling through eastern Europe to Constantinople and then through Asia Minor to Palestine.

These routes were mountain free but posed other hazards, such as bandits, war, and civil unrest. In 1064, a large group of pilgrims led by Gunther, Bishop of Bamberg, set out from Bavaria, traveling through Hungary, the Byzantine Empire, and Syria. Gunther reports being harassed and attacked continuously by local populations, culminating in an all-out siege near Ramla. Some historians surmise that the bishop invited this trouble by traveling ostentatiously rather than humbly, in the true spirit of a pilgrim. Nevertheless, given these kinds of problems with the overland route, later pilgrims deemed it safer to go through Venice and from there to cross the Mediterranean Sea to the Holy Land. This itinerary forced pilgrims coming from England and northern Europe to surmount the Alps, which formed a natural obstacle on the road to Italy.

Medieval travelers peppered their logs and journals with remarks about the Alps. One twelfth-century monk named John de Bremble at first thought that standing atop an Alpine peak might bring him closer to heaven but then decided it was more like hell: "The marble pavement of the rocky ground is ice, and you cannot safely set a foot down." Sometimes, hell is a sheet of ice rather than a burning fire. Master de Bremble then describes a further inconvenience that strikes fear into the heart of this writer as I set down the words of this chapter. Addressing his superior at the monastery, he says, "I put my hand in my scrip to scratch out a word or two to your sincerity: behold I found my ink-bottle filled with a dry mass of ice . . . I could not write."

John de Bremble (eventually) scratched out his message while on a business trip for his monastery, but each pilgrim faced similar difficulties. Looking at the itinerary of our companion mystic Margery Kempe, we see she encountered the Alps on her pilgrimage to Jerusalem in 1413. She took a fairly typical route to the Holy Land. First, she and her company sailed from Great Yarmouth in East Anglia to the Dutch town of Zierikzee. From there, they either sailed up the Rhine River or traveled overland through the Holy Roman Empire to the city of Konstanz in southern Germany. This leg of the journey was a good seven hundred miles.

Margery's journey was one of detour and challenge. She had to skirt the entire country of France due to Franco-Burgundian conflicts that threatened to erupt into civil war. And during her journey through the Holy Roman Empire, she endured the mounting hostility of her traveling companions, who objected to what they characterized as Margery's overly pious behavior. They resented her "talk of holiness" and her abstaining from meat and also seemed nonplussed that those they met along the way held Margery in high regard. Margery's companions finally abandoned her in Konstanz, even preventing her maidservant from continuing the journey with her. That meant Margery had to face the Alps alone.

Picture yourself in Margery's place for a moment. You've just walked seven hundred miles with people you don't like, and you're not even halfway to Jerusalem. Arriving in Konstanz, you look up and see the Alps. They've been visible for some time as you walked. At first they were little more than a blue haze in the distance, but now each snow-capped peak is clearly silhouetted against the sky. The mountains are beautiful. Majestic. Deadly. Now imagine you will have to surmount these peaks. There is no way around. You must go over.

Medieval pilgrims did not scale the mountains with ice picks or ropes. They took established Alpine passes and hired local guides. Some of the passes they walked are still trodden today, including the Great Saint Bernard Pass, the most ancient Alpine road and one of the highest. This pass connects Switzerland and Italy, skirting the majestic Mont Blanc. Today it is mostly a scenic route, but in the Middle Ages, the hazards outweighed the views, leading the Italian monk Saint Bernard of Menthon to build a hospice at its highest point in the mid-eleventh century.

These passes and hostels still did not domesticate the Alps. Crossing the mountains remained one of the most adventurous and hazardous legs of medieval pilgrimage. In 1436, the Spanish traveler Pero Tafur visited Jerusalem as a pilgrim and journeyed widely from there, eventually taking the Saint Gotthard Pass in central Switzerland. He describes his Alpine crossing and the dangers involved:

It was the end of August when the snow melts
by reason of the great heat, and the crossing
is therefore very perilous. The people in those
parts have oxen which are accustomed to the
way. One of these beasts goes in front drawing
a long rope, and attached to the rope is a trailer
which resembles a Castilian threshing machine.
On this the passenger sits, holding his horse
behind him by the reins, and the crossing is thus
safely accomplished, for if anything untow-
ard occurs, only the ox is imperilled. In pass-
ing along narrow ways, where the snow which
covers the mountains on either side threatens to
fall, the people discharge fire-arms so that the
report may bring down any snow which is ready
to be dislodged. For it happens at times that the
snow becomes loosened and buries travellers.

Alpine passes were especially dangerous in the
winter, when temperatures plummeted and snowfall could exceed sixty feet. In December 1128,
Rudolph, abbot of Saint Trond in Belgium, traveled
with a group of pilgrims on the Great Saint Bernard
Pass. A heavy snowfall stranded them in the small
village of Saint Rémy. "In this place, as in the jaws of
death, we remained huddled together day and night
in peril of death," Rudolph wrote. During their stay

and again as they prepared to leave, a series of ava-
lanches took the lives of several pilgrims and guides
in their traveling party.

Three centuries later, Margery Kempe crossed the
Alps, likely taking the same Great Saint Bernard Pass.
She seems to have fared better than Rudolph's pilgrims; she survived the journey, at any rate. Margery's
written report of her Alpine crossing at first seems
puzzling. A loquacious writer, she didn't hesitate to
inform readers about certain travel challenges, such
as her mistreatment by fellow pilgrims. Yet there's a
strange lack of detail about the physical mountains
that barred her way. Reading her account, we find her
one moment in Konstanz and the next in Bologna.
In between these two cities—in the silence of her
narrative—lie the Alps.

Each pilgrim putting pen to parchment speaks
with a unique voice. While some, like Rudolph of
Saint Trond, give a sense of the journey's adventure,
Margery prefers to lavish detail on people, relationships, and inner transformation. As we'll see later in
our journey, she spends many words on her mysti-
cal vision in Jerusalem. Although she doesn't make a
clear statement on the point, we can surmise that her
experience in the holy city made her Alpine crossing
entirely worth it. She willingly surmounted all kinds
of obstacles on her way to Jesus.

We who walk our faith to Jerusalem are certain to meet our own set of obstacles. We encounter the challenges of the road even when we bring along our spiritual practices, such as prayer or contemplation. For prayer is its own pilgrimage and a mountainous way. It transforms us into travelers who walk a steep and winding path. When we pause to pray or meditate, we leave behind our surroundings in the outer world, with its unceasing clamor, and journey to what Saint Bonaventure called the interior Jerusalem—that place deep within where Jesus awaits. In its own way, the inner road to Jerusalem is as demanding as the physical quest of the Alps.

Medieval mystics and theologians remark on the challenges of prayer so frequently that it is a wonder any of us attempt this inner journey. In his commentary on 1 Corinthians, Saint Thomas Aquinas, with a touch of dry humor, comments on our human failings when attempting even the briefest of prayers: "It is hardly possible to say a single 'Our Father,'" he writes, "without our minds wandering off to other things."

Most of us feel the sting of recognition in this remark. We try to take the mountainous paths of the inner journey, only to be lured off the road by the challenge or the chattering voices in our head—an internal, distracting noise Buddhists call the "monkey mind."

The anonymous author of *The Cloud of Unknowing* writes about the noise of those incessant thoughts. These thoughts will press down on you, he says, and try to keep you from praying: "It's also true that because of our own selfish wills, we forever fight distraction, always contending with thoughts of others and situations wedging themselves between us and God." These thoughts are especially troublesome to beginners in the practice of silent or contemplative prayer, the *Cloud* author notes. Yet reading his treatise, one gets the sense that all of us are and always will be beginners. Our mountainous way may never become straight. The *Cloud* author, a seasoned monk and mystic, admits he himself has not mastered the way of prayer. His counsel is to cling to our desire for God, for this is sometimes all we have: "Longing to pray is praying, and without that the soul is dead."

None of us possess the spiritual mastery to surmount the obstacles that suddenly arise like mountains in our inner landscape: anxiety, willfulness, anger, doubt. But Jesus, the one we meet in Jerusalem, does.

And as medieval pilgrims and mystics braved the Alps, we too may find that our own way becomes passable.

What will help us is not mastery or strenuous effort, but faith. Jesus once told his followers, "If you have faith as small as a mustard seed, you can say to this mountain, 'Move from here to there,' and it will move. Nothing," Jesus added, "will be impossible for you" (Matthew 17:20 NIV). A faith that moves mountains is something medieval pilgrims surely understood. In fact, some pilgrims put it on their list of things to pack for the journey to Jerusalem. The fifteenth-century Italian pilgrim Pietro Casola advised, "Each one who goes on the voyage to the Sepulchre of our Lord has need of three sacks—a sack of patience, a sack of money and a sack of faith." That's not your ordinary packing list.

Pietro's juxtaposition of money and faith is not without humor—another sack that may be necessary for a lengthy journey. Yet he is serious about the need for faith. In his travel journal, he notes that for Jerusalem pilgrims, "it is necessary to open the third sack, called the sack of faith, otherwise the voyage would be made in vain." Without faith, there would be no way to surmount the hardships of pilgrimage. And as Santo Brasca reminded us in chapter 3, faith also provides the best motive for undertaking such a voyage. A true pilgrim journeys not out of ambition or curiosity, but from a deep desire to meet the mystery of Jesus in Jerusalem. Faith is at once the pilgrim's goal *and* her means of reaching it. All who take this road need a deep sack filled to overflowing with this essential virtue.

Faith is what we discover when we approach the Alps alongside our pilgrim guides. These pilgrims had to have faith that they could make it over the mountains. Faith that their destination lay on the other side. Faith that their arduous journey would be worthwhile in the end. A sack of faith turned those on pilgrimage into mountain climbers, sometimes despite themselves.

Some days, I wonder if faith will carry me to the end of the road. The obstacles loom so large. A few months ago, I faced one of the most difficult decisions I've ever had to make. The decision would affect my spiritual health and determine my path through life. With prayer, discernment, and accompanying self-doubt, I realized, with a sense of foreboding, that the road I needed to take led through the iciest Alpine pass I could imagine. My destination lay on the other side; there was no other way to reach it than by the mountain pass. So I began the ascent. Companions held my hand, but it did not seem enough. I was tired, so tired, of climbing; I never wanted to be a mountaineer. One day I wept with a friend. "I don't understand why this road has to be so steep," I said through streaming tears. I still don't understand. I have no answers, only two companions: the knowledge that this mountainous way is indeed my path and, often, a crushing doubt that wonders if my pilgrimage is worth trying to survive it.

When travelers are struggling on the spiritual road, they need to dig into their supplies, hoping they had the foresight to pack enough for the journey. Yet frequently, as in my Alpine crossing, we find our sack of faith depleted. Mentors and fellow pilgrims can lend us some of theirs, reminding us of what is good and true about our journey. I know that I cannot climb my own mountains without sister- and brother-wanderers by my side. We also have a guide who invites us to approach him with our every need. In the Gospels, people with empty sacks often asked Jesus for the faith they lacked. Jesus's disciples begged him, "Increase our faith!" (Luke 17:5 NIV). One pilgrim from the Gospels said to Jesus, "I do believe; help me overcome my unbelief!" (Mark 9:24 NIV).

Even those followers of Jesus who traveled the roads of Palestine with him, who prayed with him, listened to his teaching, and were healed by his hands— even they had to ask for faith. They never seemed to have enough.

Our faith isn't something we can dredge up on our own or hoard in sufficient quantities to see us all the way through. As we go on our way, we need to keep returning to the source. We might find it worthwhile to pause frequently and pray the short prayer from the Gospel of Mark: "I believe; help my unbelief!" Asking for what we lack, we find our sack replenished from a supply that never runs out.

Sometimes, admitting that we don't have what we need is the only way to take steps to Jerusalem. On our spiritual journey, we don't have mastery; we don't even possess enough belief. We can only rest on the mountain pass and turn to Jesus, trusting that our sack will be filled with a faith that crosses and—sometimes—moves mountains.

THE NARROW WAY

IS FITS AND STARTS

# 6

# Hurry Up and Wait

aving crossed the Alps, Margery Kempe made her way from Bologna to Venice, arriving in early 1414. There she waited thirteen weeks for a boat to take her to the Holy Land. She was not alone in meeting with delays. For most pilgrims, Venice introduced a caesura, or pause, in their journey to Jerusalem. Coming from towns across England and Europe, they stopped in the port city to plan the rest of their voyage. "Pilgrims often arrived in Venice with plenty of time to spare," notes scholar Charity Scott Stokes, partly because they did not know the precise departure date of the sailing galleys. But in Margery's case, "time to spare" turned into "loads of extra time." Pilgrims hurried across the Alps only to wait.

Margery doesn't remark on the length of her Venetian caesura. We know that she took Communion every Sunday in a large nunnery, perhaps the Benedictine convent of San Zaccaria. And she was ill in that time. At least one scholar believes that Margery gave birth to her fourteenth child while in Venice and either left the baby in the care of a wet nurse or took the infant with her—in which case her forced sojourn was a blessing rather than a bane. Better to give birth on land than aboard a sailing galley.

Whether one needed midwives, physicians, or simply distractions, there were worse places to be stuck than Venice. The gateway to the East, it was a cosmopolitan city with a population of 100,000 in Margery's day. As those on pilgrimage waited for galleys to sail in late spring or early summer, they were present for some of the city's biggest religious celebrations of the year. And Venice knew how to put on a celebration. Of special magnificence was the procession on Corpus Christi, as were the displays and feasts during Pentecost and the Ascension.

Venice was known for wedding the sacred and the secular. On Ascension Day, a unique ceremony known as the Marriage of the Sea took place. The doge of Venice, accompanied by some five thousand vessels, sailed out of the harbor and cast a ring into the Adriatic Sea to "wed" it as a show of the city's maritime power. When Friar Felix Fabri arrived in Venice in the spring of 1483, he watched the ceremony from his own hired boat. The following day, Felix and his friends rowed to a monastery, where they kissed the body of Saint Barbara, along with other relics. Later that day, the ninth of their caesura, the pilgrims enjoyed a secular pleasure: they paid an entrance fee to see an elephant, "a huge and terrible animal" that performed tricks for its keeper.

As those on pilgrimage entered the city, they also had practical tasks to complete. Preparing to cross the Mediterranean Sea, they changed currency and sought provisions for the next leg of the journey. Pilgrimage was something of an industry for the Venetians, and local guides took travelers in hand the moment they arrived, directing them to housing, helping them exchange money, and protecting their rights. The Senate carefully regulated the galleys and their owners, allowing pilgrims the opportunity to inspect the ships before choosing one for the sea crossing. Pilgrims would then sign a contract, paying the *patronus* (shipmaster) for round-trip passage, meals, protection, and, upon arrival in the Holy Land, safe-conducts, tolls, and ground transportation. In essence, they bought a travel package.

The weeks in Venice thus became, for pilgrims, a time of preparation and a time of waiting. And after the crossing of the Alps, the weeks spent there offered a much needed rest. Yet this time also introduced tension to their sacred quest. Pilgrims' longed-for destination lay beyond the body of water visible nearly everywhere in the port city of Venice. Yet their goal seemed inaccessible. These travelers stood on the cusp of the next adventurous leg of their journey when the whole enterprise, which was not fast moving to begin with, suddenly ground to a halt.

When I first read about the Venetian caesura, I thought of the "slow" movements that have blossomed in the last few decades. The Slow Food movement led the way in the 1980s. The movement encourages a return to clean food produced in local communities, eschewing the one-minute meal options of many modern kitchens. Now it has been joined by Slow Cities, Slow Fashion, and Slow Living, among others. Perhaps my favorite slow movement pertains to writing. A few years ago, author Leslie Leyland Fields wrote a

"Slow-Writing Revolt" in which she calls for harried writers to take a step back: "Slow down. M a r i n a t e. Wait. Sometimes even—stop. Sometimes even—say No." Otherwise, she says, we will lose our way. We're wasting words when we write quickly rather than passionately and well.

In a similar vein, C. Christopher Smith, with John Pattison, recently wrote a Slow Church manifesto. The authors advocate for church communities not prompted by the need for quick results but focused on the long arc of God's redemptive work in our world. We may be in a hurry, but God is not, Smith and Pattison write. God takes the long view.

Our medieval travelers were slow-movement philosophers way before the modern era. For pilgrimage, true pilgrimage, is always slow. It takes the time it needs. It meanders. It is maddeningly roundabout, and sometimes it simply stops. In fact, the journeys of Margery, Felix, and their companions have led me to dub pilgrims the inefficiency experts of the travel world.

But sometimes, inefficiency allows the shyer virtues to shine—patience, for example. We may hesitate to invest in this virtue because we want quick results, even in our spiritual journey. Or we're simply eager to get going. But pilgrims packed plenty of patience when they set out. We recall the Italian canon Pietro Casola, who took three sacks on his trip to Jerusalem: "a sack of patience, a sack of money and a sack of faith." Pilgrims held up in Venice or at other points along the way needed the sack of patience they had the foresight to take with them. However, as we'll see later on, even Pietro himself didn't pack quite enough of this virtue for some of the trials to come.

Medieval mystics—both those who pilgrimaged to Jerusalem and those who wrote about spiritual pilgrimage—emphasized patience. The fourteenth-century monk-author of *The Cloud of Unknowing*, for example, counseled a religious novice to trust in slow, transformational grace. God's work is so incremental that its movements sometimes cannot be discerned. "Grace is rarely in a rush," he says. "It touches and changes us, but usually not as soon or as suddenly as we'd like." These are good words for a novice preparing for a lifetime of sitting in silence with God and also for those of us on a journey that sometimes grinds into low gear.

Being prone to a fast-track mind-set, I find myself chafing at the *Cloud* author's counsel. Intellectually,

I can appreciate the "slow" movements and the wisdom of the mystics, but it's not easy to put this advice into practice. As I go along, I grumble, *It took me* how long *to catch on to that little lesson God tried to teach me? What do you mean it is a* life's *spiritual journey to reach Jerusalem?* One of the struggles of the walk of faith, or at least of mine, is the pace. For those who long to go forward in the love of Jesus, it can be dismaying to know that a s-l-o-o-o-o-w road stretches before us.

Impatience is not just a twenty-first-century issue, and what we feel on our pilgrim path is understandable and even biblical. In the book of Romans, Paul describes the frustration that often marks our way forward. "We know that the whole creation has been groaning as in the pains of childbirth right up to the present time," Paul writes. "Not only so, but we ourselves, who have the firstfruits of the Spirit, groan inwardly as we wait eagerly for our adoption to sonship, the redemption of our bodies. For in this hope we were saved" (Romans 8:22–24a NIV).

Our journey holds within it a groaning as we long for Jesus and look for the life to come. Holy impatience, holy longing, marks our route. We might even feel envious when others seem to move more quickly than we do. I respond with some wistfulness, for example, when I read Saint Augustine's advice for spiritual travelers. "I implore you to love with me and, by believing, to run with me," he writes. My heart is in the right place, but with apologies to the Doctor of Grace, sometimes all I can do is limp rather than run. I am learning to accept the slower pace my journey demands.

Pilgrims like Margery Kempe and Felix Fabri assure us that not everyone crosses the finish line at a dead run. Maybe we're not even supposed to. Smith and Pattison, writing about Slow Church, believe that walking or limping is more than acceptable. If we think of the Christian faith as a journey, its path, Smith and Pattison say, meanders:

> The narrow way is fits and starts. It's running and walking and sometimes waiting. It's mountains and valleys and darkness and light. It's not being able to see the nose on our own faces and then things suddenly opening up into a magnificent vista. It's sometimes hard, but adventures usually are. It's not efficient; it's a conversation. You're more likely to go three miles an hour than seventy. You may feel alone but you're not. God is there. And look around you: a great cloud of witnesses.

Maybe we should slow down and enjoy the company.

One witness in this great cloud—Saint Ignatius of Loyola—gives us insight into the purpose of spiritual inefficiency. Yes, Ignatius takes us into the Renaissance period, but his story is influenced by the cloud of the Middle Ages. Born into a noble family in 1491, Ignatius at first followed the fast track to success. He trained for a court and military career and was so eager to achieve glory that at age thirty he pushed for an ill-advised resistance against the French army in the Battle of Pamplona. There he was badly wounded. As he convalesced in his ancestral castle in Loyola, he perused some spiritual readings, among them stories of medieval saints and mystics, that prompted him to make a complete break with his previous life. He decided that his new path should begin with a pilgrimage to Jerusalem. And he set his feet in that direction—making plans, selling his clothing, and referring to himself as "the pilgrim."

On the way to Barcelona to sail for Italy and the Holy Land, Ignatius took a detour to the Spanish town of Manresa to further prepare for his pilgrimage. The detour lasted eleven months. We're not completely sure why Ignatius was delayed so long. Some scholars believe that he couldn't sail out of Barcelona due to reports of plague in the city. Whatever the cause, God used this "slow" time to form him. While in Manresa, Ignatius spent several hours each day praying alone in a cave, as well as attending Mass, reading, and writing. "God treated him at this time just as a schoolmaster treats a child whom he is teaching," Ignatius wrote of this experience. What he learned in this waiting time, in this school for the soul, became part of the groundwork of his *Spiritual Exercises* (published in 1548), an influential book of Christian formation.

Ignatius finally made it to Jerusalem on September 4, 1523, over a year and a half after beginning his journey. But his experience in Manresa had so molded him that he pilgrimed as a contemplative rather than as a convert. Referring to himself as "the pilgrim," he writes, "On seeing the city the pilgrim felt great consolation; and as the others testified, this was common to them all, with a joy that did not seem natural. He always felt this same devotion on his visits to the holy places." Ignatius was so prepared to soak up the gifts of the Holy Land that once he arrived, he never wanted to leave. In fact, he made plans to stay but had to return to Spain under threat of excommunication from the Guardians of Mount Zion (who did not allow pilgrims to remain for the long term).

From Ignatius's experience, we learn that waiting might be a more active posture than we thought. It is, or can be, a time of growth, of soaking up lessons, of preparation for what is to come. And it reminds us again of Pietro Casola's recommendation for every pilgrim: a sack of patience. Priest and author Henri Nouwen once wrote an article on the spirituality of waiting: "A waiting person is a patient person," Nouwen says. "The word 'patience' means the willingness to stay where we are and live the situation out to the full in the belief that something hidden there will manifest itself to us."

In the waiting, we might acquire the tool or growth we need for the next leg of our journey. If Ignatius hadn't taken his lengthy detour on the way to Jerusalem, he would not have been as prepared to receive the unnatural joy God granted him in the Holy Land. And he might never have written the *Spiritual Exercises*, a work that has formed generations of Christians. In our own caesura, an equally big epiphany might come our way. Or some small but essential gift. So it's good to be attentive to the work God is doing in the present moment. In parts of the *Spiritual Exercises*, Ignatius invites us to think and pray about where we've seen God presently, for example in our daily path. Sometimes, a single day's work is enough for us to absorb.

Ignatius's journey to Manresa is sometimes called the Ignatian Way, just as the more popular Camino de Santiago is called the Way of Saint James. I think it's time we learned to follow this way: to cool our heels, be present where we are, maybe even live in a cave for a while. We need to let God do God's work in us.

Despite the lengthy delay, Ignatius of Loyola eventually got on a ship to the Holy Land. So did Margery Kempe. And so will we. Following in the footsteps of these pilgrims, we can wait—and learn and grow and allow ourselves to be formed by the slow work of the master—if our sack is filled with the patience this journey requires.

we sail
toward god

# 7

# Sail the Sea

In 1480, the pilgrim Santo Brasca traveled to Venice en route to the Holy Land. Speeding around the city, he bought supplies for the journey ahead, focusing on the upcoming sea crossing. In his travel guide, he later reflected on his experiences, advising future pilgrims bound for Jerusalem. Would-be pilgrims preparing to sail, Santo writes, should be sure to take:

- A thin mattress
- A floor-length overcoat
- A night-stool or covered pail
- A long chest
- Barrels for water and wine

Food items should include sugar loaves and a supply of good Lombard cheese. Santo goes on, "Above all, travelers should have with them a great deal of fruit syrup, because that is what keeps a person alive in the great heat; and also syrup of ginger to settle the stomach if it should be upset by excessive vomiting, but the ginger should be used sparingly, because it is very heating."

The more supplies the better, for before reaching the Holy Land, pilgrims spent some five weeks in a galley plying the waters of the Mediterranean Sea. Having crossed the Alps and then cooled their heels in Venice, sometimes for a long while, they were ready for the next leg of their journey. On the other side of all that water, the Holy Land awaited.

When the time for departure came, pilgrims boarded their galley, a large ship outfitted with both sails and oars. Below the deck, the hold contained a dormitory, where passengers slept and stored their belongings. Each pilgrim was allotted one and one-half feet for a mattress. In his guide, Santo urges pilgrims to arrive at the ship early to claim a decent berth near a source of fresh air. An English pilgrim named William Wey echoes this advice: "Choose for yourself a place in the said galley on the highest deck, because below, in the lowest, it is right smouldering hot and stinking."

Then to sea. After weighing anchor in front of the Doge's Palace, the galley carried pilgrims on the five-week journey to Jaffa, a port city on the coast of historic Palestine. The typical route took them to ports of call along the Dalmatian coast, such as Zadar and Ragusa (Dubrovnik), and then on to the Greek Islands of Corfu, Rhodes, and Crete. The general route from Venice to the Holy Land can be seen on the map in this book. Although the galleys stopped often, the sea crossing loomed large in pilgrims' minds. Friar Felix Fabri devotes several chapters of his travel guide to the Mediterranean Sea—its origins, its saltiness, and its relationship to the "Ocean" that "runs round the world." Felix refers to the Mediterranean as the Great Sea or "our sea."

By "our sea," Felix does not imply affection. As we recall from chapter 4, Felix dreaded the sea crossing, a leg of the journey that tempted him to abandon his pilgrimage. For him and many other pilgrims, sailing introduced a new form of travel and a need for renewed faith. When pilgrims boarded their galley, no longer did they put one foot in front of the other. They entrusted themselves to an entity that seemed almost alive, that would bear them to the Holy Land with little control on their part except for the exchange of money and fervent prayers. The sea invited pilgrims into unfamiliar territory long before their arrival on a distant coast.

Indeed, the Great Sea seemed to make its own rules that could be neither controlled nor predicted. Pilgrims' accounts often mention its capricious ways. The galley would sail along briskly, one pilgrim would write, only to suddenly be blown off course by contrary winds. Or the pilot would lose his way and have to backtrack or reroute the vessel. Entering the open sea proved to be particularly unnerving. Surrounded by water and sky, pilgrims strained their eyes to catch sight of any hazy form that would resolve into a coastline. Pietro Casola describes a day on his sea crossing when no land was to be seen in any direction, causing the crew to begin a "considerable war of words" about whether or not the galley was on the right course.

But it was. The day wore on, until at the twentieth hour, a lookout finally spotted the towers of Jaffa. The Holy Land was in sight.

"Be prepared for what lies ahead" has been the motto for my own spiritual journey. I'm the kind of pilgrim that boards her ship well provisioned and ready to meet the waters that will carry me forward. Like Felix

Fabri, I've done my research on the Great Sea. Like Santo Brasca, I've laid in supplies. In fact, I've probably bought the complete travel package—mules, guides, and all. Holy Land, here I come.

Yet no matter how prepared I am for this pilgrimage, at some point I can count on entering territory in which all the familiar landmarks dissolve in a haze, as in the open sea. Suddenly, I can no longer see my way forward. I cannot even be sure that I'm headed in the right direction. The Trappist monk and writer Thomas Merton gave voice to this feeling of disorientation in his well-known prayer that begins, "My Lord God, I have no idea where I am going. I do not see the road ahead of me. I cannot know for certain where it will end." This is a prayer Father James Martin recommended "everyone can pray," and no wonder. We all travel, sometimes anxiously and blindly, through life's many unknowns.

Merton's prayer continues as he reflects on further uncertainties in his path:

> Nor do I really know myself, and the fact that I think I am following your will does not mean that I am actually doing so. But I believe that the desire to please you does in fact please you. And I hope I have that desire in all that I am doing. I hope that I will never do anything apart from that desire. And I know that if I do this you will

lead me by the right road, though I may know nothing about it.

In expressing these unknowns, Merton sounds a good deal like a mystic from the Middle Ages, a period whose writers he read deeply. The medieval monk-author of *The Cloud of Unknowing*, for example, similarly commented on our inability to see everything or even most things about our spiritual pilgrimage. When we take the journey of contemplative, or silent, prayer, the *Cloud* author writes, we must be willing to do so in a kind of darkness. We can reach out to God, but there will always be a cloud separating us from the divine. This "unknowing" applies not just to the novice but also to the longtime contemplative. It is part of the journey of spiritual pilgrimage, because so much about the God we love remains shrouded in mystery. "You'll never see anything very clearly in this life," the *Cloud* author warns, "but you can certainly grope your way toward God."

Later in the book, the *Cloud* author remarks that we "sail" toward God. The change of metaphor evokes the sea crossing of our medieval pilgrims. Of the contemplative life, the author writes, "You're in a little ship crossing a vast spiritual ocean, leaving behind your focus on the physical and heading toward the life of the spirit." The sea crossing this monk describes is nothing less than a journey of transformation. The vast and rolling ocean evokes a space of becoming, one with no solid ground in sight. In this space, we constantly change as we grow, learn, make mistakes, and undertake course corrections—that is, as we mature in our journey of faith. We're heading to a distant shore that, when we arrive, will witness the full flowering of a soul made perfect in Christ. But—we're not there yet.

On board a galley, medieval pilgrims must have asked a thousand times, "Are we there yet?" Five weeks on a crowded ship introduced travelers to experiences that tested their faith, their sanity, and their stomachs. At sea, pilgrims had a more or less set routine that included meals, recreation, and daily prayers. Unfortunately, they also had to make time each day for tasks like catching lice and vermin. Fleas, mice, and rats swarmed their cramped sleeping quarters at night. And, Felix reports, exhausted pilgrims were known to throw the contents of their chamber pots at burning lights to put them out. The more unsavory aspects of human nature tended to be intensified at sea, wrote Felix.

Just as frustrating as the nightlife were the vicissitudes of nature. Pilgrims describe the alternations between the absence of wind, making progress impossible, and violent storms that threatened to break apart the ship. In travel accounts, pilgrims seem to classify each tempest as the worst they have ever encountered. Traveling to Jerusalem in 1419, the French pilgrim Nompar of Caumont describes a storm in which objects and men were thrown about the ship, which listed so badly that the mast touched the surging water. As the ship was driven toward a great rock, Nompar was sure that the end was near: "And I, seeing the sailors' expressions, you need not ask if it gave me comfort! I soon confessed and commended my soul to God and the Virgin Mary, praying that they would have pity and mercy on me in their compassion. And what shall I say? Things had reached such a pass that I no longer considered my body of any account." After barely surviving the sea's wrath and finding a safe harbor in Sicily, Nompar wrote a long prayer of thanksgiving that included many supplications for deliverance on the remainder of his voyage.

Pietro Casola survived a similar storm on his pilgrimage, concluding, in retrospect, "I believed surely that I had done what I had often talked publicly of doing and laughed at the idea—that is, chosen a fish for my sepulchre." The timing of this storm is interesting, for just two days earlier, in the port city of Ragusa, Pietro and his companions had heard a sermon comparing the Christian faith to a ship. The preacher made specific references to the pilgrims' galley: "And he concluded by saying that whoever wished to be saved must enter with Christ in this ship."

Perhaps this preacher was forewarning the pilgrims of storms like the one Pietro's galley endured just two days later. Spiritual texts of the time often give such warnings, comparing the journey of faith to weathering a stormy sea. We see one example in a fourteenth-century allegorical poem, *The Pilgrimage of Human Life*, written by the Cistercian monk Guillaume de Deguileville. The poem describes the lifelong quest of the narrator, Pilgrim, to reach the heavenly Jerusalem. Before he sets out, Pilgrim learns the nature of his path. "You want to go to Jerusalem," his guide tells him, "and to get there you must cross the great sea. The great sea is this world, and it is full of many troubles, tempests and torments, great storms and winds."

As spiritual pilgrims, we know the storms to which Deguileville alludes: adversity, unforeseen circumstances, uncertainty in our lives and in the world. Many storms rage within us as well. Recall that according to *The Cloud of Unknowing*, the sea is a place of transformation, where we feel tossed about by the ungentle winds of spiritual growth. The sea challenges us precisely because it is a changeable, in-between space in our life. And it is a large space, one where so much of the spiritual journey is lived. We can't get home without crossing it.

Sometimes I doubt I will successfully make this crossing. Out there in the open sea, I have no sight of land, only wind-tossed waves. It's easy to feel that God has abandoned me. The pilgrim-mentors with whom we're journeying sometimes felt the same. It takes all our faith, and then some, to believe in the goodness of God amid the rolling waves. By calling on others who weather the storms with me—friends, church, and the great cloud of witnesses of times past—I am able to remember that one day, the storms will pass. One day, all will be well and the good work begun in me will be brought to completion. On the sea, in the cloud of unknowing, I hold on to this truth like an anchor—although one that has been hoisted so that my ship can speed on its way. And I sail on in faith and sometimes doubt, reaching out for a land I cannot see.

Saint Augustine paints a picture of someone a little like me in his *Homilies on the Gospel of John*. Imagine a person trying to cross the sea to reach home, Augustine says. This person spots her destination from afar; she longs to reach it. In fact, all of us have this longing, for in our home country, the

One we love awaits. But how will the pilgrim get there? How will she survive the turbulent waters? How will any of us? "So that we might also have the means to go," writes Augustine, "the one we were longing to go to came here from there. And what did he make? A wooden raft for us to cross the sea on." A raft might seem a bit rickety for the raging sea, but Augustine explains: "For no one can cross the sea of this world unless carried over it on the cross of Christ."

These words bring us to one of the great paradoxes of pilgrimage. On our journey, our every step and every water crossing takes us slowly but inevitably to the heavenly Jerusalem. Yet as we make this pilgrimage *to* God, we also make it *with* God. We are not left to find our way alone, for God is at once our destination and our means of reaching it. I never tire of sifting this beautiful paradox through my mind. For those on the spiritual journey, it is a comfort to ponder the mystery that the God to whom we travel is in the boat with us—perhaps is even the boat itself.

Felix Fabri, who so feared sailing and who extensively researched the Mediterranean Sea, made two round-trip pilgrimages to the Holy Land. This meant he endured the storms, rats, and chamber pots not once, but four separate times. On his sea voyage to Jerusalem in the spring of 1483, he describes the increasing fervor with which the pilgrims waited to spot land as they neared the coast of Jaffa. Felix was so excited that he couldn't eat or sleep. He and his fellow travelers bribed the sailors to keep a constant lookout, promising a gift to the one who first spotted land.

At dawn on the first day of July, a watchman finally cried out, "My lords and pilgrims, rise up and come on deck; behold, the land which you long to see is in sight!"

Much thanksgiving, prayer, and singing ensued on the galley.

The pilgrims' rejoicing reminds me of the promise that awaits us in our sea crossing. As surely as the tides roll in and out, the sea of transformation will take us to the Holy Land. We haven't arrived yet, but we have a strong boat to keep us on course and provide shelter from the storms.

Arrival

JAFFA

make the journey
from exile to pilgrim

# 8

# Be Exiled

After a difficult sea crossing, beset with many storms, Pietro Casola and the 169 pilgrims with whom he traveled docked in Jaffa, the port city in historic Palestine and gateway to the Holy Land. The sailing portion of their voyage had come to a much-anticipated end. As they neared land, the pilgrims sang the *Te Deum Laudamus* (O God, We Praise You) and prepared to press on toward Jerusalem. But for an additional two weeks, most of them were not allowed to leave the galley.

Stuck on board the ship, Pietro and his companions were prey to an unfortunate and common part of medieval pilgrimage: delay by an administrative snafu. The pilgrims could not disembark until they obtained safe-conducts from the local officials. And no officials presented themselves.

Behind this delay lies the fraught history of the Holy Land. When Pietro and his fellow pilgrims docked in Jaffa, they prepared to enter contested territory. At one time, the West had controlled Jerusalem and its environs, establishing four Crusader states. But from the late thirteenth century, the Mamluk sultans had sole jurisdiction over the Holy Land. Western pilgrims were tolerated, if not warmly welcomed, by the sultan, and the relationship between the two cultures remained tense. Consequently, when pilgrims like Pietro neared the sacred terrain they'd traveled so far to see, they found the way to be difficult and sometimes barred.

When Pietro's galley entered the Jaffa harbor, a scribe went ashore with a letter for the governors of Ramla and Jerusalem, asking for permission to enter the Holy Land. But the pilgrims were told they must wait for the governor of Gaza to arrive. And he took his time.

Stuck in his ship, Pietro grew increasingly frustrated. He had just traversed Italy, waited in Venice, and crossed the stormy waters. All that remained of his journey was the final leg, in which the pilgrims would ride by donkey the approximately thirty miles from Jaffa to Jerusalem. He could see the Holy Land from his galley—yet he could not step foot there.

Pilgrims reacted in varying ways to such delays, just as we do in our travels today. Faced with a snag on a long-distance trip, some of us patiently settle in with a book and a cup of coffee. Or perhaps we endure long lines at customer service in hopes of getting an earlier resolution. Although not pleased by the holdup, Pietro's party tried to pass the time amiably by giving and listening to sermons, fishing, and watching giant sea turtles swim around their boat.

Yet Pietro reveals his true feelings in the travel account he wrote following this pilgrimage. In its pages, he waxes poetic about the snafu that kept him from his journey. Somewhat of an intellectual, he first turns to mythology, comparing his plight to that of Tantalus, one of the sons of Zeus. Tantalus endured a punishment that resonated with Pietro, given the sea in which the pilgrims were marooned: "Nevertheless we remained, like they say Tantalus does in the Inferno. He has the water up to his lips and cannot drink. We saw the land we had come so far to enter, and the Moors would not let us go on our way."

Then Pietro settles on an even more memorable image, writing that his ordeal felt "as hard as exile and very cruel." Describing each exhausting day of being held aboard his ship, he returns again and again to this image. He and his companions, Pietro insists, are exiles. Exile is a striking, even a loaded, term for Pietro to employ. Traveling as a self-defined pilgrim, he suddenly embraces a different identity. If a pilgrim has a difficult journey, the exile has it to a new extreme. Pilgrims always have a destination in sight, but exiles have no place to go; they are temporarily or forever denied a homeland. Given how the human heart yearns for home, it is an especially cruel condition that leaves the condemned adrift, unable to move forward or to retreat.

As a churchman, Pietro would have used this term in light of its scriptural connotations, especially the Babylonian Exile of 597–581 BCE. After King Nebuchadnezzar besieged Jerusalem and destroyed the temple, thousands of Israelites were deported to Babylon. One psalm of lament records the desolation of their exile:

> By the rivers of Babylon we sat and wept
>     when we remembered Zion.
> There on the poplars
>     we hung our harps,
> for there our captors asked us for songs,
>     our tormentors demanded songs of joy;
>     they said, "Sing us one of the songs of Zion!"

> How can we sing the songs of the Lord
>> while in a foreign land?
> If I forget you, Jerusalem,
>> may my right hand forget its skill.
> May my tongue cling to the roof of my mouth
>> if I do not remember you,
> if I do not consider Jerusalem
>> my highest joy. (Psalm 137:1–6 NIV)

Pietro would also have been familiar with the exile of his countryman Dante Alighieri. A politician as well as a poet, Dante was banished from his native city of Florence when a rival political party seized power in 1302. He gives voice to his exile in the *Convivio*:

> I have traveled through nearly all the regions where this language reaches, a wanderer, practically begging, showing the wound of fortune despite myself, the wound which so often is unjustly imputed to the one who is wounded. Truly I have been a boat without sail or rudder, carried to various ports and inlets and shores by the dry wind that painful poverty blows.

From 1302 until his death in 1321, Dante traveled the Italian peninsula, seeking refuge. Describing his exile, he uses the terms *wandering, wounded, begging, poverty*. And he ends with the unforgettable image of a boat without sail or rudder. This is the language of exile, the description of someone without a home. This was indeed how the pilgrim Pietro Casola described himself as he waited in his own boat at the Jaffa harbor, neither here nor there, longing for his "home" country.

In light of the Babylonian Exile and Dante's forever banishment, Pietro's cooption of the term *exile* seems extreme. He appears to have forgotten all about the sack of patience he advised pilgrims to pack for their journey. But perhaps we can forgive him his hyperbole, as we all understand what it is like to work toward a suddenly unobtainable goal. In our lives, we frequently go through what feel like exiles or mini-exiles: when we lose a job, experience the loss of love, or struggle through the dark night of depression. Or we endure a season of spiritual dryness that leaves us feeling stunted in our relationship with God.

Our sense of exile might at times be more profound, reaching into the core of who we are. Even when things are going well, dis-ease lurks beneath the surface of our contentment. Author Jen Pollock Michel writes, "Each of us—however happily settled—suffers a foreboding sense of rupture, as if we have been cut off from some hidden source of happiness." Something that we can't quite identify is lacking.

When trouble comes, our unease can be especially acute. This feeling can be difficult to put into words, but my friend Helen captures the frustration well when she exclaims, "We were made for the garden!"—referring to the momentous event that barred Adam and Eve from their earthly paradise.

As people of faith, and fundamentally as human beings, we are all exiles from Eden, our first and true home. We were meant to live naked, unashamed, surrounded by beauty, and in complete intimacy with our Creator. We were made for the garden. Instead, we wander the world, barred from the one place we belong.

Our exile manifests itself in many ways. As we wander, we know sorrow, sickness, political oppression, and strife. We grieve the bitter road that is ours to walk. It should have been otherwise. I long for it to have been otherwise. In a letter to his son written in 1945, author J. R. R. Tolkien says, "We all long for [Eden], and we are constantly glimpsing it: our whole nature at its best and least corrupted, its gentlest and most humane, is still soaked with the sense of 'exile.'" The grief that we feel is part of our history, a symptom of our shared humanity. And something would be desperately wrong if we did *not* long for our lost home.

Humanity's ache for Eden was so profound in the Middle Ages that many Christians sought a literal glimpse of the garden, which they referred to as Earthly Paradise. They plotted Paradise on their maps, and after giving it a physical location, tried to reach this elusive site. Their travel accounts reveal an adventurous spirit and an urge to explore the world. Beneath the curiosity, however, lies a deeply seated desire to go home again. Some of these accounts are heartbreaking in their beauty and longing. In the late fourteenth century, a Dutch cleric named Johannes de Hese claimed that he glimpsed Paradise from a distance as he traveled through the Far East. Johannes wrote, "And around the hour of vespers, when the sun goes down . . . the wall of Paradise can be seen in great clarity and beauty, like a star."

Our aching and searching may yet serve a purpose. As Tolkien implies in his letter, our yearning for Eden is the best part of our human nature. It's the part that remembers home; the part that remembers how we were meant to live. Author Michelle Van Loon adds that our yearning serves the additional purpose of acting as a compass, showing us the way forward. Exile, she reminds us, is not our permanent lot. It is not our final destination. Instead, "exile is meant to transform us into pilgrims."

We will always have a bit of the exile lodged within us, yet we are ultimately called to make the turn to a pilgrim identity. As people of God, we journey with faith and hope, knowing that a sure destination awaits us. Even the most traumatic events in our history can be understood as opportunities to go forward. Dante the exile, for instance, became Dante the pilgrim in his best-known work, *The Divine Comedy*. The poem takes Dante (or his alter ego) on a journey from the dark woods of despair all the way home, where he finds a "love that moves the sun and other stars."

Even Adam and Eve, banished from the garden at the beginning of human history, have the sure hope of coming home. As we've seen from Tolkien and others, their banishment often is viewed as a definitive exile. Yet one medieval author, the German historian Otto of Friesing, saw it another way. In his universal chronicle, *The Two Cities*, he writes that Adam was cast from the garden "into this pilgrimage." Otto sees the long expanse of Christian history, from the expulsion from Eden to the New Jerusalem, as a pilgrimage rather than an exile. Humankind may have been cast from the garden. Yet at the very moment of our expulsion, we began making the long journey home.

Our medieval traveler Pietro Casola found himself making this journey in miniature. After a two-week exile in the harbor at Jaffa, he and his fellow pilgrims finally were granted permission to enter the Holy Land. When the good news came, Pietro gathered his bags, disembarked from the galley, and after clearing a few more administrative hurdles, prepared to continue on his way. At last, the day came. On August 1, the pilgrims were given mounts and set out at vespers in the direction of Jerusalem. Pietro left exile behind and became a pilgrim once more.

Our own journeys might share similar shifts in identity, especially as we think about particular seasons of our spiritual life. Considering where we've been and where we stand now, we're likely to see periods of both exile and pilgrimage. In frustrating times, we may be tempted to shout, "Exile!" Perhaps it seems like all we do is wander without getting anywhere; roadblocks bar the way. In these times, we might pause and remember that the landscape in which we find ourselves is not just a place of exile. It is also the place of our pilgrimage. The barren earth we wander can become a verdant land in which we once again catch sight of the path that will lead us forward. Taking small steps and gazing toward a distant horizon, we make the journey from exile to pilgrim.

I try to intentionally take this journey in my own life. Sometimes I begin my morning by saying, "I am a pilgrim today." This affirmation helps me claim my true identity and move into the day with hope. I also consider the witness of medieval pilgrims like Pietro Casola. Their desire and perseverance show us that there is a way forward. Despite hardship, setbacks, and exile, God's people can complete their journey.

Yes, Pietro the pilgrim completed his journey. After finally leaving the ship, he mounted a mule and continued on his way to Jerusalem. Even so, his further travels were not without mishap. He got sunburned, slept rough, and on the road from Ramla to Jerusalem hit a stone as he fell off his mule, sustaining serious injuries to his arm and foot. Still, he pressed on. On

August 5, 1494, two and a half months after leaving his hometown of Milan, he arrived in Jerusalem.

In the spirit of Pietro and our other pilgrim mentors, we can take courage to press on in our own journeys. We can make the turn from exile to pilgrim. If we are lost, we can reorient ourselves, turning our feet toward the Holy Land once more. If we are stalled, we take a step. If we are alienated, we ask someone to journey with us. Wherever we are, we are invited, always, to rejoin the pilgrim path.

we arrive with nothing so that jesus can give us everything

# Arrive Naked

In the Middle Ages, every pilgrimage came at a cost. The physical cost soared as travelers pushed themselves to journey in extreme weather and terrain. The emotional cost mounted as they battled homesickness and disorientation. The spiritual cost rose as they suffered, following a sense of call for their faith. Pilgrimage took a toll on both body and soul.

But some costs were of a more practical nature.

The fact is, pilgrimages cost money—as anyone who's taken a lengthy trip surely understands. Those who journeyed to Jerusalem had to buy provisions, pay for passage to the Holy Land, and provide for dependents and holdings left at home. By some estimates, a pilgrimage to Jerusalem required a year's income. This daunting sum troubled nearly every traveler. Our three pilgrim mentors—Felix Fabri, Margery Kempe, and Pietro Casola—all worried about money and hoped that the lack of it would not prevent their journey beyond the sea.

When Felix resolved to go to Jerusalem in 1480, he had several hurdles to overcome. His first worry was about obtaining permission from his order to travel. His next hurdle seemed even more difficult. "Nor could I form any idea of how I should raise the money for such an expensive journey," he wrote. Seeing his fervent desire for pilgrimage, two superiors in his order gave him not only leave to travel but also money for the trip.

When Margery heard Jesus directing her to visit Jerusalem (along with Rome and Santiago), her thoughts likewise turned to funds. "Where shall I get the money with which to go to all these holy places?" she asked Jesus. In her writings, she records that the Lord replied, "I shall send you friends enough in the various parts of England to help you." And she did find help. During Margery's visit to Lincoln, the bishop, Philip Repyndon, provided her with money for her pilgrimage in exchange for her prayers. Margery also used an inheritance from her father to pay her husband's debts and settle her own, ensuring permission to depart.

Pietro fretted about money throughout his 1494 Jerusalem pilgrimage. After being exiled on his sailing galley for fifteen days, he created his maxim for pilgrims that we've seen a couple of times already: "Each one who goes on the voyage to the Sepulchre of our Lord has need of three sacks—a sack of patience, a sack of money and a sack of faith." In his travel journal, Pietro notes occasions on which the pilgrims dipped into their sacks of patience and faith. And as they waited for local officials to give them permission to enter the Holy Land, they tried *not* to dip into their sack of money: "The Moors made difficulties, now about one thing, now about another, as they had never done before, from what I could hear from those who had been there on previous occasions. However, it was necessary to tie everything up in the sack of patience, as we did not want to loosen the sack of money."

Dipping into the money sack might have moved things along, but Pietro did not want to bribe the officials and so deplete the pilgrims' funds. Readers of his story sometimes get the impression that money was a far scarcer and more valuable resource than either patience or faith. Yet the pilgrims did finally loosen their sacks of coins, notably for those in need of medical attention for heatstroke on the road from Ramla to Jerusalem.

Pilgrims also opened their sacks for tolls, which often proved to be a hardship. Travel diaries reveal that pilgrims paid tolls when they first arrived in the Holy Land, at checkpoints in Jaffa and Ramla, and again when they entered Jerusalem. Additional fees had to be paid to enter the Holy Sepulchre itself. In the later Middle Ages, some of these tolls and fees were included as part of the travel package pilgrims purchased from Venetian shipmasters.

Having spent a good deal of money on their voyage, and possibly more than budgeted due to unforeseen delays, some pilgrims arrived in Jerusalem without the necessary funds in their sack. This shortage threw the outcome of their pilgrimage into doubt and put their lives in danger. In 1346, a Franciscan pilgrim was threatened with flogging and imprisonment for being unable to pay the poll tax, the money required for non-Muslim visitors to enter Jerusalem. Another fourteenth-century pilgrim warns that those who traveled penniless might lose their life or be required to renounce their faith.

Margery herself resorted to begging after she left Jerusalem and made a further pilgrimage to Rome. She reports that the Lord asked her to give away all her money, which she did. Until her return to England,

Margery relied on the hospitality of others for food and shelter and begged door to door when necessary.

Unfortunate scenes played out earlier in the Middle Ages as well. Writing in the late twelfth century, the chronicler William of Tyre describes a group of pilgrims who had come to Jerusalem to worship at the holy sites: "But the keepers of the gates refused them admittance until they should pay the gold piece which was fixed as tribute money. Those who had lost their all upon the way, however, and had with extreme difficulty arrived in physical safety at their longed for goal, had nothing with which to pay tribute. So it happened that more than 1000 pilgrims, who had gathered before the city to await the privilege of entering, died of hunger and nakedness."

A popular story relates that when Robert, duke of Normandy (the father of William the Conqueror), encountered one such group of penniless pilgrims in 1036, he took pity and paid the tribute for them.

These stories of desperate travelers call into question the whole enterprise of pilgrimage. Imagine taking the long and grueling journey to the Holy Land—having planned your trip, saved up money, crossed the Alps, and sailed the sea—only to be denied entrance to Jerusalem due to lack of money. This common occurrence raises difficult questions. What happened to pilgrims who did not find a sponsor to pay their toll? If pilgrims could not afford to even enter the city, how were they able to fund their voyage home?

There's an old adage that pilgrims should carry few possessions and depend upon the hospitality of others, as did Margery during her visit to Rome. But what if a pilgrim's poverty prevents her from reaching the very destination of her journey?

These questions do not become easier to answer when we consider our spiritual pilgrimage. Like the physical traveler, we who walk in faith today can expect the costs to be high. Whether we embark on a way of prayer or the long road of life, we may arrive at our destination with insufficient resources. Walter Hilton, the English mystic who has occasionally offered mentorship to us on this journey, says we should plan our pilgrimage with poverty in mind. In *The Scale of Perfection*, he prescribes scarcity for all who take the journey to their interior Jerusalem: "Just as a true pilgrim leaves behind him house and land, spouse and children, and makes himself poor and bare of all that he has in order to travel light and without hindrance, so if you want to be a spiritual pilgrim you are to make yourself naked of all that you have."

In this passage from the book, Hilton first describes the destitution of a *physical* pilgrim. He lists all that a "true pilgrim" must leave behind—house, land, and family—and describes the pilgrim's financial state— poor. Then he explains why this must be the case. Pilgrims make themselves poor in order to remove barriers. With less to carry, they are fleet of foot.

We get this advice from contemporary pilgrims, too. Reading through websites and message boards aimed at preparing travelers for a lengthy journey, I've observed that the common formula is something like this:

1. Pack your bag.
2. Take out half of what you packed.

Those who overdo it find themselves shedding belongings as they walk. Phileena Heuertz describes the process of letting go as she embarked on the Camino de Santiago a few years ago: "I had to leave behind everything but what I thought would be essential for the journey. And then even along the way I had to shed a number of items in my pack that were weighing me down and threatening to impede my journey and keep me from reaching Santiago."

In the same way, too much internal baggage can impede arrival at our spiritual destination. That's why Hilton cautions spiritual pilgrims to travel light. Of course, this does not come naturally to most of us. As pilgrims on a journey of faith, we're apt to tote around all kinds of cumbersome loads. Some baggage we might find beneficial, such as the sacks of patience and faith Pietro Casola advised us to pack. Yet many a spiritual pilgrim has been known to leave these virtues behind in favor of other, less useful items. Pilgrims, Hilton says, often carry around the deeds they have done, whether good or bad. They rely on good works to lighten the load, or they carry the weight of guilt over their mistakes and misdeeds.

The temptation to pack this kind of luggage is understandable; you and I have surely carried this much and more on our spiritual journey. Yet excess weight merely distracts us from our goal—"Jesus, alone," as Hilton says. We can become so busy juggling our good and bad works that they fully occupy our mind; Jesus himself is all but forgotten. Encumbered by the weight we were never meant to carry, we are slowed to a crawl, and our destination recedes further into the distance.

So we must learn to let go. But as Walter Hilton says in his advice to pilgrims, we leave behind more than our possessions. The spiritual pilgrim, in a sense, always travels naked.

Medieval mystics frequently tout the virtues of stripping naked. This word—*naked*—arrests us, makes us pause. It's almost certainly not the term we ourselves would choose when discussing our spiritual state. Yet the mystics embraced it. It is one of their preferred ways to describe the shedding of layers that obscure our true motives or our true self. The author of *The Cloud of Unknowing* writes of meeting God with "naked intent," which he defines as a "simple reaching out to God for himself." Naked intent means approaching God in prayer, especially contemplative prayer, without expectation of any reward or benefit—that is, with only the desire to know God. To let go of other motivations, we discard layers of worldly attachments as a physical pilgrim sheds clothing or a heavy scrip.

Just before introducing his pilgrimage parable, Hilton discusses another form of spiritual nakedness. He describes the necessity of our soul becoming "naked of all good works," of acknowledging our poverty and nothingness before God. Acceptance of our nothingness is one of Hilton's favorite themes, as expressed in the mantra we learned in chapter 4: "I am nothing; I have nothing; I desire nothing but the love of Jesus alone." Only when we are stripped of all that falsely shores us up can our soul stand naked before Jesus with a pure motive and clear vision.

Marguerite Porete, a thirteenth-century French mystic, writes of this nakedness, too, in *The Mirror of Simple Souls*. Porete describes the journey of a soul who becomes subsumed by and within divine Love. On this journey, the soul relinquishes her will and comes to discover her own nothingness, which reveals her to be "naked without covering." But such nakedness does not shame the soul; it shows her, by way of contrast, the power and goodness of God. And it offers her a great gift: "These showings make the soul deep, large, supreme, and sure. For they make her always naked, All and Nothing, as long as they hold her in their embrace."

For the spiritual pilgrim, "Nothing" leads to "All." In our nakedness, we are embraced and clothed by the warmth and goodness of God.

Getting naked is difficult work; it's certainly not for the faint of heart. It can be uncomfortable to strip in front of the mirror's assessing gaze and even more so before our maker, who sees everything. Nakedness means being willing for God to see us for who we really are. It means acknowledging our own nothingness before God. It means making ourselves bare of ulterior motives and reaching out to God with no expectation of material blessings or "good feelings" in return.

I don't relish the idea of traveling naked, because I am not a light packer. When I set out on my spiritual journey, I usually begin with a full backpack. I stuff in all my good works, my self-improvements, and my promises to do better. I pick up my pack and test it. It's heavy, but usually I can find room for a few more items. In go my justifications, explanations, and excuses. My pack sags with the weight of all my possessions, but it is almost unthinkable to set off without them. Jesus will want to see these valuable spiritual items, I reason. He will want to see my good works; I will want him to see my excuses for the times I failed to perform them.

Yet Hilton and other mystics seem to think that Jesus will not want our spiritual baggage. Travel poor, the mystics urge. Go all the way to Jesus, upend your sack, and show him there is nothing inside. No self-justifications. No shiny good works to pay the entrance fee. Don't hide behind your bulging sacks. Stand exposed. Naked. Needy.

Contemplating our nakedness, undoubtedly with some trepidation, we are guided by the stories of two medieval pilgrims. We met the first in chapter 7, in Guillaume de Deguileville's poem, *The Pilgrimage of Human Life*. The poem relates the journey of a spiritual pilgrim who must cross the Great Sea. At the end of his journey, Pilgrim finally arrives at the heavenly Jerusalem and stands before its gates. But he cannot yet enter. His guide has a final word of instruction for him: "If you are stripped naked you will be received within."

Pilgrim didn't arrive at Jerusalem with much but surrendered the little he did have. He entered heaven's gates with absolutely nothing. It was the only way he *could* enter.

Deguileville's allegorical pilgrim mirrors the story of a medieval saint who stripped naked before his village, his human father, and his God. The saint's name is Francis of Assisi, the thirteenth-century Italian friar. Saint Francis began life with wealth and privilege but, at the beginning of his public ministry, renounced his inheritance with a dramatic gesture: he removed his fine clothing in front of the bishop and all who surrounded him. Francis's biographer, Saint Bonaventure, wrote that he "even took off his underwear."

Throughout his ministry, Francis continued to strip down. He frequently gave away his clothing and material goods. At the end of his life, he desired to die naked in order to be like Christ, who hung naked on the cross in poverty and pain. Bonaventure writes of him:

In all things
Francis wished to be conformed to Christ
     crucified,
who hung on the cross
poor, suffering and naked,
Therefore at the beginning of his conversion,
he stood naked before the bishop,
and at the end of his life,
naked he wished to go out of this world.
He enjoined the friars assisting him,
under obedience and charity,
that when they saw he was dead,
they should allow
his body to lie naked on the ground
for the length of time
it takes to walk a leisurely mile.

For Francis, becoming poor and naked was inextricably tied to his spiritual journey. He thought of himself as a pilgrim and an exile, and that meant embracing a life of poverty. Bonaventure says that

Francis instructed the friars of his order to build humble homes and to live in them "not as their own, but like *pilgrims and strangers* in the house of another. For he used to say that the law of pilgrims was to take shelter under another's roof, to thirst for their homeland, and to travel peacefully."

Deguileville's pilgrim and his real-life counterpart, Saint Francis, teach us one of the most baffling lessons of pilgrimage. The world tells us to accrue more and more as we go along in life. Even on our spiritual journey, we're supposed to acquire more: more answers, more wisdom, more faith, more (spiritual) wealth. The pilgrim's way, by contrast, is a way of letting go. Only by accepting and then embracing our poverty will we reach our destination. Standing before God with nothing, not even the clothes on our back, we have not failed; we have finally and fully arrived.

"The goal of all spirituality is to lead the 'naked person' to stand trustfully before the naked God," writes Franciscan friar Richard Rohr. "The important thing is that we're naked; in other words, that we come without title, shame, merit, or even demerit." Coming empty to the cross, we begin to trust God to give us what we need. We are filled with God's spirit rather than our own false resources or our lack.

If we stand naked before God, Rohr continues, it also means we have nothing to give God—no offering, no gifts, nothing God really wants or needs. How challenging it is to come empty-handed to the king. This is a further emptying of our self, Rohr writes. "All we can offer to God is who we really are, which to all of us never seems like enough."

When we finally stagger into Jerusalem, poor and spent, it is likely we will not have enough to pay the entrance fee. We must rely on Jesus to pay the toll for us. This he does, giving us what we cannot supply ourselves: merit, forgiveness, grace, and all the treasures of heaven.

Standing naked before the cross, with nothing on our back and nothing in our sack, we learn the lesson of every destitute pilgrim. To journey to Jerusalem is to arrive with nothing so that Jesus can give us everything.

ENTER a TERRAIN MADE SACRED BY THE FOOTSTEPS OF JESUS

# 10

## Worship with the Enemy

L o, here is the city of the Great King, whose likeness all the Churches of the world are not able to present," wrote a German pilgrim named John Poloner, who traveled to the Holy Land in 1421. Usually taciturn throughout his travel guide, John waxes poetic in describing the city at the center of the known world. And many other pilgrims do the same. After a journey over land and sea, by foot, sailing galley, and mule, the first glimpse of that long-awaited destination could be emotional. The pilgrims had finally arrived. They were in Jerusalem.

With little delay, a tour of the city's sacred sites commenced. As we visit these sites with our pilgrim guides, we'll encounter places familiar to us from the New Testament and Christian tradition. Becoming pilgrims ourselves, we will pause at the Mount of Olives and the Way of Sorrows, the Golden Gate and the House of Pilate. Seeing these places through the eyes of medieval travelers opens us to a new view of the Holy Land and of our inner landscape of faith.

A medieval pilgrim's visit to Jerusalem centered on places in the lives of Jesus, Mary, and the saints, with an emphasis on those related to the passion of Christ. Pilgrims toured the sites as a group and went to each in a particular order. In the following list, the English pilgrim William Wey describes his tour of Jerusalem in 1462. Some of the sites he mentions are related to the life of Mary and the teachings and healing miracles of Jesus. Most, however, form part of the Way of Sorrows, the path of Jesus from his condemnation to the cross (William does not describe these sites in the order of the Passion narrative, however). The pilgrims saw, William writes:

> First the stone with the crosses where Christ fell;
> Second, the street where Christ carried His cross;
> Third, the home of the rich man who was
> damned;
> Fourth, the crossroads where Christ fell with
> His cross;

Fifth, the place where the women wept over
Christ;

Sixth, where Veronica took Christ's face in her
handkerchief;

Seventh, where the Most Blessed Virgin Mary
fainted;

Eighth, the gate through which Christ was led
to death;

Ninth, the pool where the sick were healed
when the waters were disturbed;

Tenth, the two white stones in the wall above
the heads of passers-by on which Jesus stood
when he was condemned to death by Pilate;

Eleventh, the school of the Blessed Mary where
she learned her letters.

Along that street, on the other side, is Pilate's
house, where Christ was flogged and condemned to death.

Then we visited the other places in Jerusalem.

The "other places" to which William refers included
Calvary and the Holy Sepulchre, where we'll later
linger with our pilgrims.

Pilgrims also visited places associated with Jesus's
public ministry. One important site, the Mount of
Olives, has been revered by Jewish and Christian worshippers for centuries. Located near Jerusalem's Old
City, it hosts an ancient Jewish cemetery. In the New

Testament, Jesus delivered some of his teachings on the Mount of Olives and went there to pray following the Last Supper. Some in the Christian tradition have identified a cave on this mountain as the place where Jesus taught his disciples the Lord's Prayer. When a twelfth-century German pilgrim named Theoderich visited the cave, he noted that many pilgrims kissed the surface upon which Jesus wrote the words to this prayer.

Jerusalem's landscape invited embodied responses, many of which went beyond the mere touching or kissing of sacred sites. Some pilgrims, after seeing the column to which Jesus was bound when he was scourged, were themselves moved to be scourged in imitation of their Lord. Others went barefoot while in Jerusalem or threw themselves down in fits of ecstasy upon seeing one or another sacred site.

Perhaps the most unusual somatic response comes from a pilgrim traveling with Friar Felix Fabri. Near the cave on the Mount of Olives stood a chapel enclosing the site of Christ's ascension. Here, Felix says, the Savior's footprints could be clearly seen pressed into a rock, "though the print of the right foot is the plainer of the two." Pilgrims often kissed the rock, but one worshipper was so moved that he poured sweet wine, of which he carried some in a flask, into the footprints, and the other pilgrims licked it out. "And as fast as the place was emptied he poured more in," marvels Felix.

In instances like this, Jerusalem surely exceeded the hopes and expectations of pilgrims. Licking wine from the Savior's footprints! What other experience could give them such an intimate taste of Jesus's humanity?

Yet Jerusalem sometimes came as a disappointment to visitors. When pilgrims like William Wey and Felix Fabri entered the gates of this city at the center of the world, they did not just meet Jesus. They also encountered those of other faiths, whom they considered to be obstacles to their physical and spiritual journey. As rulers of the Holy Land from 1291, the Egyptian and Mamluk sultans controlled access to its sacred sites. Some of the holy places were off limits to Western visitors; others were contested; still others had been destroyed. Jerusalem did not fully belong to the pilgrims who had journeyed so far to see it. Its glory existed in fragments, in history, and in dreams, but not as a lived reality.

At the same place Friar Felix observed the wine poured in the footprints of Jesus, he notes that there once stood a beautiful church honoring Christ's ascension. The church had first been turned into a mosque and subsequently was torn down, save for the chapel enclosing Christ's footprints—a sacred site for both Muslim and Christian worshippers. Thus, as pilgrims stood on the Mount of Olives, they experienced loss as well as awe.

Destroyed, too, was the church called Saint Mary of the Swoon, where Mary fainted when she saw Jesus carrying his cross. Only some of its walls remained. Every attempt to build another structure on those walls, legend said, had been unsuccessful. For Felix, this proved the sanctity of the original site.

And destruction, it should be noted, was also caused by pilgrims themselves, who wanted to take home bits and pieces of the Holy Land. Felix observes that the imprint of Jesus's knees on the Mount of Olives was no longer visible because pilgrims had chipped away at the rock. One group of pilgrims scandalized the Eastern Christians when they broke off pieces of the Holy Sepulchre and the rock of Calvary. The Father Guardian of Mount Zion immediately excommunicated all who had done so.

Some holy sites, although still standing, had been turned by each new conquest of Jerusalem into mosques or madrassas. Such was the case with the

Church of Saint Anne, the Tomb of King David on Mount Zion, the House of King Herod, and what pilgrims believed to be Solomon's Temple. An important place in Jesus's life, the Golden Gate, was also off limits. According to Christian tradition, Jesus entered Jerusalem by this gate on Palm Sunday. However, a Muslim burial site lay nearby, so Christians were forbidden to approach the gate.

As pilgrims made the rounds, seeing some sites and barred from others, they were guided by Franciscan friars, the only Western Christians who permanently resided in Jerusalem. Considered to be custodians of the holy sites, the Franciscans alone had authority to conduct tours. They also organized the pilgrims' lodging, liaised with local officials, and helped sick travelers. Even as they provided a valuable service, almost like an all-inclusive travel package, their constant presence reminded pilgrims that freedom of movement was not in the offing while in the Holy Land.

Unless, that is, the pilgrim's name was Felix Fabri. Having come the long way to Jerusalem, our Dominican friend was determined to visit all the places he could, with or without permission. Citing the rule that no pilgrim should wander around without a guide, he sheepishly admits, "I, Brother Felix Fabri, did not observe this article strictly, as will appear hereafter."

Felix, for example, found a way to sneak into the Tomb of David (which had been made into a mosque) on Mount Zion:

> The keeper of the mosque trying one day to shut the door quickly, hampered the lock with the key, so that the key would not move the iron bolt; so he went away leaving the mosque open: and it remained open as long as I was in Jerusalem, and more than ten times I have gone into it and looked round it, though I always went in and came out with fear and trembling, because if any Saracen had seen me there I should have come into great trouble, even had I escaped from the peril of death.

At other times, the Muslim guardians of the holy sites helped him enter forbidden places. Felix was able to see the House of Pilate, which had become a dwelling for a Muslim family, when the two daughters of the house let him in. As the location of Jesus's trial and condemnation, Pilate's House was a significant site along the Way of Sorrows. It contained a round, vaulted chapel marking the place where Jesus was scourged. In Felix's day, this chapel was a place in which the current residents of the house threw dirt and refuse. However, Felix did not hesitate to get down into the dirt and pray.

When Felix went to the Holy Land, Pilate's House was largely inaccessible to Western visitors. In fact, Felix boasts that not one in a thousand pilgrims could gain access. But Felix was more enterprising than most. He appears to have made a deal with the two "good-looking, rather tall girls" who lived in the house that he and his companions could go in whenever the girls' father was away.

Clearly, Felix had a complicated relationship with his Muslim hosts. He was not above sneaking into their sacred sites or striking deals to see others. Yet sometimes he befriended the locals. On his 1483 journey, he had a joyful reunion with the Muslim man, named Cassa, who had provided him a donkey on his previous pilgrimage. Felix presented Cassa with a gift of stirrups, and the two men spent much time together during Felix's visit to the Holy Land. They seemed to regard each other with friendship and mutual respect.

Our mystic friend Margery Kempe fostered similar relationships. She writes that while in the Holy Land, she received more kindness from her Muslim guides than from her own companions. These local guides, she says, "made much of her and escorted her and led her around the region, wherever she wished to go. And she found all the people in the Holy Land to be good and gentle towards her." Such stories are a balm amid so many accounts of distrust and animosity between Jewish, Christian, and Muslim communities.

Yet not all interactions went as well. Pietro Casola's traveling party repeatedly clashed with the Muslim guardians of Jerusalem, who believed the pilgrims to be spying on the city. And in his account, Felix recalls the time a local official chased his companions from the Fountain of the Virgin, located at the foot of Mount Zion, leading to a fistfight between the official and a Lombard knight in the pilgrims' group. Jerusalem did not always offer the vision of peace for which its visitors longed.

In his habit and tonsure, Friar Felix cuts quite a figure as he darts around Jerusalem, shaking off his guides, ducking into doorways, and striking deals. At points in his writings, he seems to be crafting an identity as an adventurer in the name of faith.

But Felix also felt frustration regarding the conflicts marking Jerusalem's sacred terrain. Toward the end of his life, he wrote a devotional manual that revises his difficult experience in the Holy Land.

Called *The Zion Pilgrim*, the manual takes readers on a vicarious journey to Jerusalem. It gave medieval worshippers, especially enclosed nuns, a way to take a pilgrimage in their spiritual life, much as our mystic friend Walter Hilton advised Christians to do. Yet the pilgrimage it offers is heavily idealized: Felix's spiritual pilgrims encounter no enemies, no closed doors, no religious or political tension at all. Instead, they serenely travel from one sacred site to another, praying freely at each one.

*The Zion Pilgrim* shows how much Felix longed for a Jerusalem that didn't exist. He dreamed of a peaceful and worshipful sojourn within the holy city's gates. But the spiritual life rarely offers such an idyllic journey. The truth is that followers of Jesus will always pass through contested territory, always encounter conflict and enemies on the Jerusalem road. Along the way, we learn an important lesson. Our truest enemies are not in the landscape "out there." They aren't people on differing political or religious spectrums or those of differing beliefs. They are likely not, in fact, people at all. For spiritual pilgrims, the greatest foes are the infidels of our own heart.

These enemies of the spiritual pilgrim sneak into all the nooks and crannies of our lives. They easily persuade our hearts to turn against us. All it takes is a memory, a destructive thought, or a glance at someone against whom we hold a grudge, and suddenly, the sacred space of our inner terrain has become a dark and treacherous minefield. In the midst of the heart, the place where God dwells, we are denied true entrance by the enemy within.

It is our mystic friend Walter Hilton who, in *The Scale of Perfection*, names these enemies. We've met some of them earlier in the book—fear, the longing for comfort, and the temptation to turn back from our pilgrimage path.

We might discover that as we approach Jerusalem, our enemies become bolder in their harassment. On my own journey, fear often whispers to me that the path is too dangerous. Then, as I travel further, a new enemy called shame saunters up and stands directly in my way. Sometimes, I feel shame over my own misdeeds, and this is a matter for confession. But more often than not, shame is a liar rather than a truth teller, an enemy that tries to convince me that I am unworthy to make the passage toward and with the love of God. How tragic it is to walk so many miles only to be stopped in my tracks by the message of divine love denied.

If these or other enemies also dog your path, fellow pilgrim, take heart. Hilton teaches us how to respond. Neither shame nor any other foe should keep us from our journey, he says. He tells us that God's love makes us worthy, and he counsels us to pray. If fear and shame continue whispering their lies to us, Hilton reminds us to reach into our scrip and pull out our mantra: *I am nothing; I have nothing; I desire nothing except the love of Jesus alone.* Those words help us retrain our gaze on our destination. They shore up our faith that we are on the path to Jesus, even though enemies breathe down our neck. Do not hesitate, beloved sister- or brother-wanderer, to repeat this mantra in troubled times. Let it refocus your heart and mind on the reason for your pilgrimage.

Heeding Hilton's advice, we also remember the challenge and promise of Scripture. When Jesus spoke to his disciples shortly before his arrest in the garden, he said words to comfort them in dark times: "In this world you will have trouble. But take heart! I have overcome the world" (John 16:33 NIV). We are called to believe and trust in Jesus even in the midst of trouble. Even in the presence of our foes.

Pilgrims like Felix, Margery, and Pietro did just that. Despite setbacks, they did not leave off their travel or worship. They kissed the holy places they could not enter. They knelt nearby if barred from a sacred site. They prayed. They sang. They read Scripture. They wept. They dug deep into their scrip for a faith that let them see past the barricades to a terrain made sacred by the footsteps of Jesus.

THE FIRE OF
LOVE
BURNS WITHIN US.

# 11

# Be Reborn

In this book, we have followed pilgrims over the Alps, across the Great Sea, and into the streets of Jerusalem. In the Holy City itself, we've walked the Way of Sorrows that marks Jesus's journey to the cross. We've lapped wine from his footprints and gotten as close as possible to every site graced by his presence. But we have not yet broached the most sacred place on our pilgrimage.

It is time now to slow our steps as we approach the Church of the Holy Sepulchre. It is time to think about why we have made this long and arduous journey. It is time to stand before Jesus himself.

Pilgrims visited and revered many sacred spaces in Jerusalem. Yet ultimately, the most precious of sites was the Church of the Holy Sepulchre, built on the place where Jesus was crucified, buried, and resurrected. Here, pilgrims encountered the presence of Christ as nowhere else. Here, their pilgrimage reached its true end. This church, housing the cross and the empty tomb, was considered the beating heart of Jerusalem and the center of medieval Christendom.

And here, wanderer-pilgrim, you too meet the journey's end, which is also a beginning. For no one walks the long road to Jerusalem and remains unchanged. So, as we visit Jerusalem's most sacred site alongside our pilgrim mentors, we look for what is being birthed in our lives, our faith, and our heart.

Approaching the Holy Sepulchre with Friar Felix Fabri, we let ourselves experience the mounting anticipation. Felix and his companions had stopped and prayed when they caught their first glimpse of Jerusalem from afar. Drawing near the city, they dismounted from their mules and entered through the Fish Gate. Before getting settled into their hostel or doing anything else, they were led down a long street and into the courtyard of a "great closed church." Only then, when the pilgrims were gathered in suspense, did a friar from Mount Zion announce that they were standing before the Church of the Holy Sepulchre.

The news set off an explosion among the pilgrims, as Felix describes: "Some knelt on the earth with their bare knees, and prayed with tears, holding their arms out in the form of a cross. Others were shaken with such violent sobs that they could not hold themselves up, and were forced to sit down and hold their heads with their hands, that they might endure their thick-coming sobs."

The pilgrims reacted dramatically and bodily. After three long months of travel—crossing the Alps, sailing the sea, bouncing along on mules, and being barred entry to the Holy Land—pilgrims had finally reached their destination; they had made it to Jesus. At several points on their three-thousand-mile journey, many of them had thought they might perish, as some of their companions did. So it is no wonder that, standing in the courtyard of the Church of the Holy Sepulchre, they had a moment of pure cathartic release.

The real highlight of their pilgrimage came a few days later, when pilgrims finally entered the church. This was no touristy visit. No, our pilgrims hadn't walked and sailed and ridden the long way to Jerusalem just to sightsee. They wanted an experience. So, by night rather than day, they went inside the Church of the Holy Sepulchre, had the door bolted behind them, and spent three nights locked up with Jesus.

When the time came for what I think of as the first church lock-in, anticipation mounted. At the hour of evensong, the pilgrims assembled in the courtyard of the church, beautifully paved with slabs of marble, as Pietro Casola recalls, and paid an entry fee of five ducats apiece. The Muslim guardians then let them in and, by previous arrangement, bolted the door behind them. "Oh how joyous an imprisonment!" Felix exclaimed when the door clanged shut. "How desirable a captivity! how delightful an enclosure! how sweet a locking in, whereby the Christian is locked in and imprisoned in the sepulchre of his Lord!"

Until daybreak, there was no way out; the pilgrims had become captives for Jesus.

Once the pilgrim-captives were locked inside the Church of the Holy Sepulchre, a well-organized vigil ensued. Margery Kempe, Felix Fabri, and Pietro Casola record that the Franciscan brethren of Mount Zion led them in a candlelit procession around the interior. They climbed up and down stairs in the maze of the church, which held many chapels, niches, and sacred caves. Felix describes the interior as "darksome," with some chapels located underground, "sunk deep among the rocks," and others little more than caverns hewn out of the rock itself. The Chapel of Saint Helena, he says, was overhung by rocks and overlooked a pit, deep and terrible, representing part of the chasm where the crosses of Jesus and the two thieves were flung after the crucifixion.

I imagine the pilgrims' candles flickering as they processed from site to site, illuminating with small points of light the somber places marking the suffering of Jesus. Sometimes the pilgrims must have asked a companion to hold their candle as they knelt in prayer or squeezed into some crevice so as not to miss any detail of this sacred place.

The pilgrims paused at each chapel to recite a brief service, sing songs, and touch or kiss the holy places. They visited at least a dozen chapels, including the cell in which Jesus had been imprisoned, Mount Calvary Chapel, and the Holy Sepulchre itself. They also saw the Church of Golgotha, located in the choir of the church, which boasted a round stone said to mark the center or navel of the world. Many a pilgrim's account makes note that all who visit Christ's sepulchre have made a journey to the very center of the earth.

Yet pilgrims saved their greatest reverence for Mount Calvary. The twelfth-century pilgrim

Theoderich writes that this chapel "shines in the church as doth the eye in the head." Indeed this chapel was brighter than many in the church, featuring polished marble, mosaics, and paintings. Theoderich records a tradition whereby pilgrims brought small crosses from their homeland and laid them atop the rock of Calvary itself. Some pilgrims also got down on all fours and plunged their head into the socket hole into which the cross of Christ had been set. The sweet scent coming from this hole, wrote Felix three centuries later, refreshed all who breathed it in.

Following the procession, pilgrims would eat meals they'd packed in their scrip and get some rest. Masses followed, some of which Felix Fabri and Pietro Casola presided over. Pietro makes note that he was able to say Mass above the Holy Sepulchre itself. Pilgrims then wandered at will throughout the church. During their "free time," Pietro touched the holy places with his rosaries, and Felix sought a quiet corner to pray through the names of friends who'd asked to be remembered in the church at the center of the world.

Following High Mass, at about eight o'clock the next morning, the captives were released. Muslim officials opened the church doors and banged on them, straining the hinges. They ran around yelling until the pilgrims, eyes blinking from the sunlight and minds still on the sacred sites within, exited into the courtyard.

Their pilgrimage through Jerusalem then continued. With virtually no sleep, the pilgrims plowed through another full day of touring Jerusalem and its environs.

Twice more, pilgrims repeated this overnight vigil in the Church of the Holy Sepulchre; together, the vigils represented an experience of death and resurrection. The pilgrims were shut in a darkened church, just as Jesus had been placed in the tomb; they followed Jesus's passion from place to place within the church; and then they emerged into the light, as had Jesus on the third day.

The very structure of this lock-in was a form of *imitatio Christi* (imitation of Christ), meant to lead pilgrims into an intimate encounter with the crucified and risen Lord.

How and where do we encounter Jesus on our own pilgrimage? Perhaps in a dimly lit sanctuary or chapel, like those in the Church of the Holy Sepulchre. At other times, it might happen in the mundane spaces of everyday life—our kitchens, workplaces, classrooms, and even our cars. Whatever our meeting place looks like, we're invited to go with an open heart and an expectation that we will be changed by the encounter.

Although not all medieval pilgrims had a heartfelt meeting with Jesus in the Church of the Holy Sepulchre, many found there a renewal of their faith. One who arrived more than ready to meet with Jesus was Margery Kempe—Margery, who had lost her traveling companions, braved the Alps alone, and waited thirteen weeks to cross the sea. This mystic's experience in the Church of the Holy Sepulchre more than made up for her troubles along the way.

During one of the nights of her lock-in with Jesus, Margery had a vision that deepened her faith. Carrying her candle and following the friars in procession, she entered Mount Calvary Chapel and immediately fell to the ground. What happened to her candle when she collapsed?, I wonder. Margery writhed and cried out, "for in the city of her soul she saw truly and freshly how our Lord was crucified." Referring to herself in the third person, she reports:

> And when, through dispensation of the high mercy of our Sovereign Saviour Christ Jesus, it was granted to this creature to behold His precious tender body so truly—all slashed and

torn with scourges, more full of holes than any dove-cote ever was, hanging on the Cross with the Crown of Thorns upon His head, His blissful hands, His tender feet nailed to the hard tree, the rivers of blood flowing out plentifully from every limb, the grisly and grievous wound in His precious side shedding forth blood and water for her love and for her salvation—then she fell down and cried out with a loud voice, marvellously twisting and writhing in her body on every side, spreading out her arms wide as if she should have died, and could not keep herself from crying and from these physical movements, due to the fire of love that burned so fervently in her soul with pure pity and compassion.

From this moment, Margery was graced with "the gift of tears," having crying spells when prompted by the contemplation of Christ's passion or "whenever God wished to send them." Margery's violent reaction astonished her onlookers and annoys modern readers, many of whom believe her tears to be a manipulation or a sign of illness. Yet Margery was not the only pilgrim to display this kind of behavior. Felix observed similar responses from the pilgrims in his party. Both inside and outside the church, pilgrims threw themselves on the ground and screamed. They wailed and groaned. They wept. Noisy demonstrations were neither uncommon nor out of place in the church at the center of the world.

Nor was Margery the only pilgrim to have visions. The fourteenth-century mystic Saint Bridget of Sweden had had a similar experience some forty years earlier. As she wept in Mount Calvary Chapel on May 14, 1372, Bridget saw Jesus being scourged and crucified. At one point, Jesus even spoke to her, noting the hole into which pilgrims thrust their heads when visiting the chapel and saying, "Pay attention, for the base of my cross was set in this hole in the rock at the time of my passion."

Not all pilgrims had visions with their bodily eyes. But most would have been accustomed to vividly imagining the sufferings of Christ. In the later Middle Ages, a certain kind of devotional text led Christians to visualize the life of Jesus as if they were by the Lord's side. One such treatise, the *Meditations on the Life of Christ*, advises, "You must direct your attention to these scenes of the Passion, as if you were actually present at the Cross; and watch the Crucifixion of our Lord with affection, diligence, love, and perseverance." As the passion unfurls, readers of the text are prompted to sorrow at Jesus's sufferings. At the scourging of Jesus, the author writes, "Here, then, consider Him diligently for a long time; and if you do not feel compassion at this point, you may count yours a heart of stone."

In the Church of the Holy Sepulchre, this affective devotion reached new heights. Pilgrims no longer just imagined scenes from Jesus's life; they were right there, standing in the place he suffered and died. The very stones spoke of Christ's passion. And pilgrims' bodies did, too, as they wept, wailed, and shrieked.

Sometimes, pilgrims' wailing sounded like suffering. Other times, it was more like the throes of birth. When his group first assembled in the courtyard of the Church of the Holy Sepulchre, Felix observed that some of the pilgrims "shrieked as though in labor." Margery herself, within the church, groaned with a kind of spiritual labor as well. Her experience in Jerusalem, says scholar Helen Hickey, marked Margery's body. Metaphorically, "she does give birth to a new Margery, one who cries loudly and uncontrollably when contemplating the sufferings of Jesus."

By her own account, Margery was reborn in Jerusalem. Not only did her expression of faith change, but her inner vision as well. After her pilgrimage, Margery reports beginning to see Jesus in the suffering of other people and even the suffering of animals. The new Margery encounters the world with a stream of tears and an outpouring of compassion, or *co-passio*: a suffering-with.

Reader, wanderer, pilgrim, here we have visited the chapels together; here we have been on pilgrimage. As our journey draws to a close, we remember that the truest pilgrimage occurs in our lives and in our hearts. Each step leads to rebirth. Saint Augustine, in the *Confessions*, writes a beautiful passage that echoes the journey of our medieval pilgrims and defines our spiritual path. Seeking divine assurance on his own journey, Augustine says to God, "I shall go into my own little room [the heart] and sing love songs to Thee, groaning unutterable groanings during my pilgrimage, recalling in my heart the Jerusalem to which my heart has been uplifted, Jerusalem my homeland, Jerusalem my mother, and Thee ruling over it." Augustine travels to his "little room"— the room of the heart—and encloses himself the way that pilgrims did in the Church of the Holy Sepulchre. And his devotions bring him to Jerusalem. A life of faith and a way of prayer, as he speaks of it, is a pilgrimage.

Augustine's groanings echo the vocalizations of pilgrims like Margery Kempe, also reborn within this church. To many, Margery and Augustine seem worlds apart in their theology, experiences, and outlook. Yet they both poured out their hearts, with groans rather than words, in the secluded settings to which they journeyed.

And we, reader-wanderers, journey to a similarly intimate space. Whatever physical surroundings we find ourselves in, perhaps we can think of our heart as a chapel to which we travel when we pray. The way is mountainous, perilous, sometimes heavily defended. Yet our perseverance and our faith allow us to finally reach this sacred space. Alone with God, our longed-for destination finally before us, we sink to the ground and rest. We drink in divine grace. And we are changed. The "fire of love," as Margery calls it, burns within us. Surely, in these moments, our faith is born anew.

Jerusalem birthed new life in our three pilgrim mentors. For Margery, the gift of pilgrimage was the fire of spiritual renewal. For Felix, it was time in solitude in a quiet corner of the Holy Sepulchre, where he remembered those who wanted their faith rebirthed by his prayers. And for Pietro, it was the honor of saying Mass above the Holy Sepulchre, celebrating the life that comes from death. Yes, pilgrimage changed these three travelers. It brought them greater intimacy with Jesus Christ and new knowledge about themselves.

On their journeys of rebirth, these pilgrims persevered. They prayed. And then they proceeded home to continue living the journey each day of their life.

This, beloved sister- and brother-wanderers, is what I trust you and I may do. I have shared to the best of my ability the journeys of medieval pilgrims through travel accounts and the pathways of my heart. And now may they keep you on your own journey. May the witness of Margery, Felix, Pietro, and the other pilgrim saints of this book speed you on your way to Jerusalem. Go in courage. Persevere. Believe. And be reborn.

# EPILOGUE

It seems almost anticlimactic to say this, but after journeying the long and winding road to Jerusalem, pilgrims then . . . turned around and went back home. We don't hear as much about their return voyage, in popular accounts anyway. It's much more exciting to learn about the journey *there*, filled with hope and anticipation, than the journey *back*, which tends to be filled with rather more exhaustion than excitement.

Pilgrims faced as many hardships on the return journey as on the way to the Holy Land. When Friar Felix Fabri departed Jerusalem after his first pilgrimage in 1480, many in his party were sick, so that the galley became "like a hospital full of wretched invalids." In fact, four pilgrims died of illness on the voyage home. In addition, the galley suffered a broken rudder and was tossed about by no fewer than four violent storms. Upon arriving in Venice, Felix himself was so ill that he remained in the care of physicians for fifteen days before traveling on to Germany. "It requires courage and audacity to attempt this pilgrimage," he concludes: "That many are prompted to it by sinful rashness and idle curiosity cannot be doubted; but to reach the holy places and to return to one's home active and well is the especial gift of God."

Margery Kempe's companions, too, faced illness on their return voyage, although she writes that God promised that none who traveled with her would die. Upon arrival in Venice, Margery was abandoned a final time: "And when our Lord had brought them back to Venice in safety, her compatriots forsook her and went away from her, leaving her alone. And some of them said that they would not travel with her for a hundred pounds." Undaunted, she continued on further pilgrimages to Assisi and Rome.

And what of our Italian friend Pietro Casola? The return sea voyage for Pietro and his companions took eight weeks instead of the usual five. They met with so many contrary winds and becalmings that the galley simply could not make progress. The pilgrims and crew ran dangerously low on provisions, and there was much murmuring against the captain for the delays. At one point, the captain ordered anyone who had brought water from the Jordan River to throw it into the sea, for it was a common belief that Jordan water brought bad luck to sailing vessels.

Sometimes the journey home was more uneventful. On Felix's second pilgrimage, the return trip went smoothly and ended on an endearing note, described by scholar Kathryne Beebe: "On 30 January 1484, more than nine months after his departure, Fabri returned to Ulm. He came just in the middle of Vespers, and no one in the convent heard him banging on the door; they were still at prayer. The convent dog, however, knew him and danced around him, rejoicing with whining and tail-wagging . . . until his brethren had finished and came out to greet his return." Felix's brothers at the convent "welcomed him as one come back from the dead." He who had been legally dying was alive once more.

A resurrection, a greeting from treasured friends, and the warm welcome of a beloved dog—it sounds a bit like heaven, doesn't it?

Our journey with medieval pilgrims has taken us over the Alps, across the sea, into exile, and deep into enemy territory. In the pathways of our heart, we've walked and sailed, been locked up and locked out, feared and had faith. Pilgrims like Felix Fabri, Margery Kempe, and Pietro Casola have proved trustworthy companions the entire way. Watching them persevere, we have learned from them what it takes to embark on a journey in our own spiritual life.

And now, as this leg of our journey ends and we close the pages of this book, may God grant you the especial gift of traveling well on your voyage of faith. The way is not easy. But I trust you have what you need to go forward. Perhaps, as happened to me, birthday candles and a trip in a metal canister will be the start of your journey. Or maybe you will hear a whisper, gentle but insistent, and decide to heed its call. However your journey begins, I hope you will respond.

May the pilgrim saints give you courage to take a new step or a first step in your journey today. As you do, recall the encouraging words of the mystic Walter Hilton: "If you keep on this way, I promise that you shall not be slain but come to the place that you desire." And remember the even dearer promise of Jesus that he has gone ahead to prepare a place for us. Will there be a dog? I honestly don't know. But I've heard tell that there are many rooms, enough for all who undertake this journey of faith. And that means that one day we'll see one another there.

# ACKNOWLEDGMENTS

No pilgrim walks alone. Companionship is one of the very great gifts of our journey. It is a pleasure to acknowledge the companions with whom I walked as I dreamed about and wrote this book. I'm grateful to those who believed in the project from the beginning, including James Catford, Ed Cyzewski, John Fea, and Michelle Van Loon. I'm also thankful to Carl McColman for conversations about medieval mystics and for listening early on to my ideas for this book, which features a mystic we both admire: Walter Hilton. My profound appreciation goes to Kelley Nikondeha, who offered valuable feedback on a draft. And running like a steady stream through all the stages of writing has been the collective wisdom and support of the Redbud Writers Guild, many members of which I met for the first time at the Calvin Festival of Faith and Writing in 2018.

I owe the greatest debt of gratitude to Lil Copan, my editor at Broadleaf. I could not have written the book without her insight and guidance. It was a joy to work with her and indeed with the entire team at Broadleaf Books.

Thank you to Paul Soupiset, who enriched this book with illustrations that add visual beauty and a meditative dimension to the journeys I narrate.

I'd also like to acknowledge the faithful companions who walked with me and nourished my soul as I wrote. They believed in me as a writer and, more importantly, as a person and a pilgrim: Marion Ahlers, Randy Blacketer, Dianne Collard, Glenn Collard, Ashley Dyson, Ailisha O'Sullivan, Tammy Perlmutter, Tina Simmons, Jessica Spears, Eric Speece, and Prasanta Verma.

Thank you, finally, to my family, especially Forrest Christian and my two beautiful daughters, Alice and Celia. I'm grateful that we walk this road side by side, with arms linked.

# MEDIEVAL VOICES

Following are the pilgrimage accounts referred to in the pages and endnotes of this book. If you're interested in hearing more from medieval pilgrims in their own voices, you may want to dip into some of these. Many of them make for excellent reading.

## Saint Bridget of Sweden

*The Revelations of St. Birgitta of Sweden.* Vol. 3, *Liber Caelestis, Books VI–VII.* Translated by Denis Searby. Oxford: Oxford University Press, 2012.

## Santo Brasca

*Canon Pietro Casola's Pilgrimage to Jerusalem in the Year 1494.* Translated by M. Margaret Newett. Manchester: University Press, 1907.

This book, though focused on Pietro Casola, contains portions of Brasca's account.

## Pietro Casola

*Canon Pietro Casola's Pilgrimage to Jerusalem in the Year 1494.* Translated by M. Margaret Newett. Manchester: University Press, 1907.

## Nompar of Caumont

*Voyaige d'Oultremer en Jhérusalem par le seigneur de Caumont* [The Overseas Voyage to Jerusalem by the Lord of Caumont]. Edited by Marquis le lièvre de la Grange. Paris: Auguste Aubry, 1858.

## Felix Fabri

*The Book of the Wanderings of Brother Felix Fabri.* Translated by Aubrey Stewart. Vols. I–II. London: Palestine Pilgrims' Text Society, 1893–96.

## Margery Kempe

*The Book of Margery Kempe.* Translated by Anthony Bale. Oxford World's Classics. Oxford: Oxford University Press, 2015.

## Moses George of Nubia

Robert of Clari. *The Conquest of Constantinople.* Translated by Edgar Holmes NcNeal. New York: Columbia University Press, 2005, pp. 79–80.

The pilgrimage account of the Nubian king who some scholars believe to have been Moses George is recorded in Robert of Clari's chronicle.

## John Poloner

*John Poloner's Description of the Holy Land (circa 1421 A.D.).* Translated by Aubrey Stewart. London: Palestine Pilgrims' Text Society, 1894.

## Pero Tafur

*Travels and Adventures, 1435–1439.* Edited and translated by Malcolm Letts. The Broadway Travellers. Reprint, New York: RoutledgeCurzon, 2005.

## Theoderich

*Theoderich's Description of the Holy Places (circa 1172 A.D.)*. Translated by Aubrey Stewart. London: Palestine Pilgrims' Text Society, 1891.

## William Wey

*The Itineraries of William Wey.* Edited and translated by Francis Davey. Oxford: Bodleian Library, 2010.

# NOTES

In this book, some historical quotations have been adapted to avoid overly gendered language and to be more accessible to contemporary readers.

## Four Pilgrimages to the Holy Land

On the map, the possible route from Nubia to Jerusalem is taken from Adam Simmons, "Uncovering the African Presence in Medieval Europe," The Public Medievalist, April 27, 2017, https://tinyurl.com/y7jy9f3a.

## Introduction

*"Keep on your way and think of Jerusalem"* and *"If you keep on this way . . . come to the place that you desire."*

Walter Hilton, *The Scale of Perfection*, trans. John P. H. Clark and Rosemary Dorward, The Classics of Western Spirituality (New York: Paulist, 1991), 227, 231 (latter quote adapted).

## Chapter 1

*"In the broad sense, a 'pilgrim' is . . . Santiago de Compostela or elsewhere."*

Dante Alighieri, *Vita Nuova* XL; translation in Julia Bolton Holloway, *The Pilgrim and the Book: A Study of Dante, Langland and Chaucer*, rev. ed., American University Studies (New York: Peter Lang, 1992), 6 (quote adapted).

*Remarking on the importance . . . "tells us we are people who spend our lives going someplace, going to God."*

Eugene H. Peterson, *A Long Obedience in the Same Direction: Discipleship in an Instant Society*, 2nd ed. (Downers Grove, IL: InterVarsity, 2000), 17.

*In addition to practical preparations . . . "furnish myself with spiritual weapons for my protection."*

*Canon Pietro Casola's Pilgrimage to Jerusalem in the Year 1494*, trans. M. Margaret Newett (Manchester: University Press, 1907), 116.

*"Now, at the end of our journey . . . glorious pilgrimage to the celestial city."*

Peter Ackroyd, *The Canterbury Tales: A Retelling* (New York: Penguin, 2009), 434.

*And on maps of the period . . . reflecting its geographical and spiritual preeminence.*

On the centrality of Jerusalem, especially on world maps of the medieval period, see my previous book: Lisa Deam,

*A World Transformed: Exploring the Spirituality of Medieval Maps* (Eugene, OR: Cascade, 2015).

*"Because you desire a practice . . . 'This is the way, and be sure to keep the instructions I give you.'"*
Walter Hilton, *The Scale of Perfection*, trans. John P. H. Clark and Rosemary Dorward, The Classics of Western Spirituality (New York: Paulist, 1991), 226–27 (quote adapted).

*Upon arrival in this place, "the true person of peace rests in the interior Jerusalem."*
Bonaventure, *The Soul's Journey into God, The Tree of Life, The Life of St. Francis*, trans. Ewert Cousins, The Classics of Western Spirituality (Mahwah, NJ: Paulist, 1978), 110 (quote adapted).

*Like the saints and other, better-known figures from history, these pilgrims are members of the great cloud of witnesses of the church eternal.*
I come to this book with a keen recognition that the survival and availability of pilgrims' accounts is often due to the lens of those who preserved (or did not preserve) this history, as well as opportunities for travel and literacy among different classes and groups of medieval people. The three travelers I've chosen to focus on represent only a piece of the pilgrimage puzzle. In particular, we are missing more women's and non-European pilgrimage voices. For the latter, good places to begin are Geraldine Heng, *The Invention of Race in the European Middle Ages* (Cambridge: Cambridge University Press, 2018); and Sergew Hable

Sellassie, *Ancient and Medieval Ethiopian History to 1270* (Addis Ababa: United Printers, 1972).

Another fruitful aspect of pilgrimage can be found in the work of theologian and social psychologist Christena Cleveland on the Black Madonnas in France and worldwide. For Cleveland's pilgrimage and virtual pilgrimage to these historical images, see Christena Cleveland, "Welcome to the Virtual Black Madonna Pilgrimage!," Patreon, January 23, 2019, https://tinyurl.com/yc88wqqg.

## Chapter 2

*"Our Lord charged her . . . that she go to Rome, to Jerusalem, and to Santiago."*

*The Book of Margery Kempe*, trans. Anthony Bale, Oxford World's Classics (Oxford: Oxford University Press, 2015), 33.

*If we look at a medieval map of the world . . . hugs the edge.*

On the Hereford Mappa Mundi, see my previous book: Lisa Deam, *A World Transformed: Exploring the Spirituality of Medieval Maps* (Eugene, OR: Cascade, 2015); and Hereford Cathedral's Mappa Mundi website, https://www.themappamundi.co.uk.

*All who go in this direction, Hilton says, take the "sure way."*

Walter Hilton, *The Scale of Perfection*, trans. John P. H. Clark and Rosemary Dorward, The Classics of Western Spirituality (New York: Paulist, 1991), 228.

*Sometimes we forget that historically, a pilgrimage almost always had an endpoint.*

A notable exception is the "aimless pilgrimage" of the medieval Irish hermits, who sometimes set out in a boat without any oars or destination or, alternatively, undertook a life of perpetual wandering and self-exile. See Jonathan Sumption, *The Age of Pilgrimage: The Medieval Journey to God* (Mahwah, NJ: HiddenSpring, 2003; orig. pub. 1975), 132–35; and Brett Edward Whalen, ed., *Pilgrimage in the Middle Ages: A Reader*, Readings in Medieval Civilizations and Cultures 16 (Toronto: University of Toronto Press, 2011), 65–70 (on the wanderings of Saint Brendan).

*The irony, Smith suggests, "is that we experience frustration . . . 'the road is life.'"*

James K. A. Smith, *On the Road with Saint Augustine: A Real-World Spirituality for Restless Hearts* (Grand Rapids: Brazos, 2019), 13, emphasis mine.

*But "never arriving means you're always leaving," writes Smith.*

James K. A. Smith, "Restless: On the Road with Augustine," *Spark* (Calvin University), June 5, 2017, https://tinyurl. com/yaudbwwx.

*When we come home, "every kind of thing will be well," as Dame Julian of Norwich writes.*

Julian of Norwich, *Showings*, trans. Edmund Colledge and James Walsh, Classics of Western Spirituality (Mahwah, NJ: Paulist, 1978), 225.

*When it comes to pilgrimage, however, "joy is arriving at the home you've never been to," writes Smith.*

Smith, *On the Road*, 47.


## Chapter 3

*"In the first place . . . receives nothing but an earthly reward."*

Quoted in *Canon Pietro Casola's Pilgrimage to Jerusalem in the Year 1494*, trans. M. Margaret Newett (Manchester: University Press, 1907), 10 (quote adapted).

*"Secondly, the pilgrim should put his affairs in order . . . may not find themselves in difficulties."*

Quoted in *Canon Pietro Casola's Pilgrimage to Jerusalem*, 10 (quote adapted).

*"One of the pilgrims . . . the third pilgrim who died before we could go to Jerusalem."*

*Canon Pietro Casola's Pilgrimage to Jerusalem*, 234.

*An even direr situation . . . only ten had made it all the way to Jerusalem.*

This story is recorded in Robert of Clari, *The Conquest of Constantinople*, trans. Edgar Holmes NcNeal (New York: Columbia University Press, 2005), 80. Robert of Clari does not name the Nubian pilgrim he mentions, but some scholars suggest that it was King Moses George. See, for example, Giovanni R. Ruffini, *Medieval Nubia: A Social and Economic History* (Oxford: Oxford University Press, 2012),

251; and Adam Simmons, "Uncovering the African Presence in Medieval Europe," The Public Medievalist, April 27, 2017, https://tinyurl.com/y7jy9f3a.

*Desert crossings . . . so that pilgrims could make a safer holy quest.*

On Ethiopian pilgrims, see Geraldine Heng, *The Invention of Race in the European Middle Ages* (Cambridge: Cambridge University Press, 2018), esp. 192; and Sergew Hable Sellassie, *Ancient and Medieval Ethiopian History to 1270* (Addis Ababa: United Printers, 1972), esp. 272–73.

*"She asked the parish priest . . . so they could consider themselves content."*

*The Book of Margery Kempe*, trans. Anthony Bale, Oxford World's Classics (Oxford: Oxford University Press, 2015), 57.

*Before leaving for Jerusalem . . . and for the resurrection of his body.*

*Voyaige d'Oultremer en Jhérusalem par le seigneur de Caumont* [The Overseas Voyage to Jerusalem by the Lord of Caumont], ed. Marquis le lièvre de la Grange (Paris: Auguste Aubry, 1858), 7–8.

*"To other humans those on pilgrimage were conventionally and legally considered to be dying."*

Celia Lewis, "Framing Fiction with Death: Chaucer's *Canterbury Tales* and the Plague," in *New Readings of Chaucer's Poetry*, ed. Robert G. Benson and Susan J. Ridyard, Chaucer Studies 31 (Cambridge: D. S. Brewer, 2003), 146.

*Pietro describes the wines . . . "although they are not so perfect as ours."*

*Canon Pietro Casola's Pilgrimage to Jerusalem*, 131.

*The knight "broke a gold ring . . . 'and after that you can marry any one you please.'"*

Dana Carleton Munro, ed., *Medieval Sermon-Stories*, Translations and Reprints from the Original Sources of European History 2, no. 4 (Philadelphia: Department of History of the University of Pennsylvania, 1901), 8.

*"We have become curators of caution rather than harbingers of hope."*

Richard Littledale, tweet posted on Twitter (Dec. 1, 2019), https://tinyurl.com/y2eb5lrw.

*As he explains the practice of spiritual pilgrimage, he introduces the parable of a man planning to go to Jerusalem.*

Walter Hilton, *The Scale of Perfection*, trans. John P. H. Clark and Rosemary Dorward, The Classics of Western Spirituality (New York: Paulist, 1991), 226–27. This is the same practice and parable introduced in chapter 1, pp. 21–22.

*"The first half of the Gospel . . . That's the whole spiritual life. It's learning how to die."*

Eugene Peterson, "Spirituality for All the Wrong Reasons," interview by Mark Galli, *Christianity Today*, March 4, 2005, https://tinyurl.com/ydy9lkam.

*"And he said that he wanted to go on pilgrimage . . . and then die there."*
Robert of Clari, *The Conquest of Constantinople*, 80.

## Chapter 4

*"There are three acts in a person's life . . . as if he were the cause of its turning out ill."*
*The Book of the Wanderings of Brother Felix Fabri*, trans. Aubrey Stewart, vol. I, pt. 1 (London: Palestine Pilgrims' Text Society, 1896), 3–4 (quote adapted).

*"After my spiritual father's departure . . . the greatest delight in doing so."*
*The Book of the Wanderings of Brother Felix Fabri*, vol. I, pt. 1, 8–9 (quote adapted).

*There are still a few intrepid people who go by foot from Europe to Jerusalem . . .*
See, for example, Mony Dojeiji and Alberto Agraso, *Walking for Peace: An Inner Journey*, rev. ed. (Walking for Peace, 2013); A. D. Dillon, *I Walked to Jerusalem: A Pilgrim's Trek Across Europe and Asia*, 2nd ed. (Manchester, UK: Azariah, 2017); and Justin Butcher, *Walking to Jerusalem: Endurance and Hope on a Pilgrimage from London to the Holy Land* (New York: Pegasus, 2019).

*"My body, mind and emotions . . . shouting for me to stop."*

Phileena Heuertz, *Pilgrimage of a Soul: Contemplative Spirituality for the Active Life*, rev. ed. (Downers Grove, IL: IVP, 2017), 80.

*In his book . . . his heart is "relentlessly committed to its many Egypts."*

Chuck DeGroat, *Leaving Egypt: Finding God in the Wilderness Places* (Grand Rapids: Square Inch, 2011), 59.

*"And therefore turn home again and leave this desire, for you will never carry it through to the end."*

Walter Hilton, *The Scale of Perfection*, trans. John P. H. Clark and Rosemary Dorward, The Classics of Western Spirituality (New York: Paulist, 1991), 231.

*"There was no intent to betray . . . I may not forget that to which my life is committed."*

Howard Thurman, *Meditations of the Heart* (Boston: Beacon, 1999), 209–10.

*"The problem is not . . . touchstones so they can sustain us during our journey."*

Christine Valters Paintner, *The Soul of a Pilgrim: Eight Practices for the Journey Within* (Notre Dame, IN: Sorin, 2015), 16.

*"I am nothing; I have nothing; I desire nothing but the love of Jesus alone."*

Hilton, *The Scale of Perfection*, 231.

*"Humility says, I am nothing; I have nothing. Love says, I desire only one thing, and that is Jesus."*

Hilton, *The Scale of Perfection*, 228.

*The author of* The Cloud of Unknowing . . . *a very simple word, such as* God.

*The Cloud of Unknowing: With the Book of Privy Counsel*, trans. Carmen Acevedo Butcher (Boston: Shambhala, 2009), 24–25.

*"I know a very beautiful sister for whom the prayer word is 'let go.'"*

M. Basil Pennington, *Centering Prayer: Renewing an Ancient Christian Prayer Form*, repr. (New York: Image, 2001), 66.

*Another prayer mantra . . . remain focused on the inner path.*

On the Jesus Prayer, see *The Way of a Pilgrim and The Pilgrim Continues on His Way* (Magdalene Press, 2015); and Frederica Mathewes-Green, *The Jesus Prayer: The Ancient Desert Prayer That Tunes the Heart to God* (Brewster, MA: Paraclete, 2009). Both the *Cloud of Unknowing* author and Mathewes-Green emphasize that there is preparatory work to do before using the prayer mantras they describe. Mathewes-Green, for example, prescribes the Jesus Prayer as part of a daily, vibrant praxis.

## Chapter 5

*"The marble pavement of the rocky ground is ice . . . I could not write."*

George B. Parks, *The English Traveler to Italy*, vol. 1 (Rome: Edizioni di Storia e Letteratura, 1954), 195.

*"It was the end of August . . . the snow becomes loosened and buries travellers."*

Pero Tafur, *Travels and Adventures, 1435–1439*, ed. and trans. Malcolm Letts, The Broadway Travellers (repr., New York: RoutledgeCurzon, 2005), 182–83.

*"In this place, as in the jaws of death, we remained huddled together day and night in peril of death."*

Parks, *The English Traveler*, 196–97.

*"It is hardly possible to say . . . without our minds wandering off to other things."*

Paul Murray, *Aquinas at Prayer: The Bible, Mysticism and Poetry* (London: Bloomsbury, 2013), 120.

*"It's also true . . . situations wedging themselves between us and God."*

*The Cloud of Unknowing: With the Book of Privy Counsel*, trans. Carmen Acevedo Butcher (Boston: Shambhala, 2009), 68–69 (quote adapted).

*"Longing to pray is praying, and without that the soul is dead."*

*The Cloud of Unknowing*, 79.

*"Each one who goes on the voyage to the Sepulchre of our Lord has need of three sacks—a sack of patience, a sack of money and a sack of faith."*

*Canon Pietro Casola's Pilgrimage to Jerusalem in the Year 1494*, trans. M. Margaret Newett (Manchester: University Press, 1907), 225.

*In his travel journal, he notes . . . "the voyage would be made in vain."*

*Canon Pietro Casola's Pilgrimage to Jerusalem*, 247.

## Chapter 6

*"Pilgrims often arrived in Venice with plenty of time to spare" . . . precise departure date of the sailing galleys.*

Charity Scott Stokes, "Margery Kempe: Her Life and the Early History of Her Book," *Mystics Quarterly* 25, no. 1/2 (1999), 32.

*At least one scholar believes . . . a blessing rather than a bane.*

Laura L. Howes, "On the Birth of Margery Kempe's Last Child," *Modern Philology* 90, no. 2 (November 1992), 220–25.

*Later that day . . . "a huge and terrible animal" that performed tricks for its keeper.*

*The Book of the Wanderings of Brother Felix Fabri*, trans. Aubrey Stewart, vol. I, pt. 1 (London: Palestine Pilgrims' Text Society, 1896), 100.

*"Slow down. M a r i n a t e. Wait. Sometimes even—stop.
Sometimes even—say No."*

Leslie Leyland Fields, "The Slow-Writing Revolt," in blog
on Leslie Leyland Fields (website), March 5, 2009, https://
tinyurl.com/yasc93fj.

*In a similar vein, C. Christopher Smith, with John Patti-
son . . . God takes the long view.*

C. Christopher Smith and John Pattison, *Slow Church: Cul-
tivating Community in the Patient Way of Jesus* (Downers
Grove, IL: IVP, 2014).

*"Grace is rarely in a rush . . . but usually not as soon or as
suddenly as we'd like."*

*The Cloud of Unknowing: With the Book of Privy Coun-
sel*, trans. Carmen Acevedo Butcher (Boston: Shambhala,
2009), 222.

*"I implore you to love with me and, by believing, to run with
me."*

Augustine of Hippo, *Commentary on the Gospel of John*;
quoted in "We Shall See Him as He Is—Augustine," Cross-
roads Initiative, August 12, 2019, https://tinyurl.com/
yd9g5abx.

*"The narrow way is fits and starts . . . And look around you:
a great cloud of witnesses."*

Smith and Pattison, *Slow Church*, 52.

*"God treated him at this time just as a schoolmaster treats a child whom he is teaching."*

*Ignatius of Loyola: Spiritual Exercises and Selected Works*, ed. George E. Ganss, Classics of Western Spirituality (New York: Paulist, 1991), 79.

*"On seeing the city . . . same devotion on his visits to the holy places."*

*Ignatius of Loyola*, 86–87.

*"A waiting person is a patient person . . . something hidden there will manifest itself to us."*

Henri J. M. Nouwen, "A Spirituality of Waiting: Being Alert to God's Presence in Our Lives," Audio CD (Notre Dame: Ave Maria, 2006).

## Chapter 7

*"Above all, travelers should have with them a great deal of fruit syrup . . . it is very heating."*

Quoted in *Canon Pietro Casola's Pilgrimage to Jerusalem in the Year 1494*, trans. M. Margaret Newett (Manchester: University Press, 1907), 11–12 (quote adapted).

*"Choose for yourself a place . . . it is right smouldering hot and stinking."*

*The Itineraries of William Wey*, ed. and trans. Francis Davey (Oxford: Bodleian Library, 2010), 26.

*After weighing anchor . . . Jaffa, a port city on the coast of historic Palestine.*

Modern-day Israel refers to the historic city of Jaffa as Yafo.

*Friar Felix Fabri devotes several chapters . . . refers to the Mediterranean as the Great Sea or "our sea."*

*The Book of the Wanderings of Brother Felix Fabri*, trans. Aubrey Stewart, vol. I, pt. 1 (London: Palestine Pilgrims' Text Society, 1896), 111.

*"My Lord God . . . I cannot know for certain where it will end."*

Thomas Merton, *Thoughts in Solitude* (New York: Farrar, Straus and Giroux, 1999; orig. pub. 1958), 79.

*This is a prayer Father James Martin recommended "everyone can pray," and no wonder.*

Trent T. Gilliss, "Thomas Merton's Prayer That Anyone Can Pray," *On Being*, December 28, 2014, https://tinyurl.com/y8n39b9y.

*"Nor do I really know myself . . . though I may know nothing about it."*

Merton, *Thoughts in Solitude*, 79.

*"You'll never see anything . . . but you can certainly grope your way toward God."*

*The Cloud of Unknowing: With the Book of Privy Counsel*, trans. Carmen Acevedo Butcher (Boston: Shambhala, 2009), 31.

*"You're in a little ship . . . heading toward the life of the spirit."*
*The Cloud of Unknowing,* 218.

*"And I, seeing the sailors' expressions . . . I no longer considered my body of any account."*
*Voyaige d'Oultremer en Jhérusalem par le seigneur de Caumont* [The Overseas Voyage to Jerusalem by the Lord of Caumont], ed. Marquis le lièvre de la Grange (Paris: Auguste Aubry, 1858), 95–96; English translation in Nicole Chareyron, *Pilgrims to Jerusalem in the Middle Ages,* trans. W. Donald Wilson (New York: Columbia University Press, 2005), 65 (quote adapted).

*"I believed surely . . . chosen a fish for my sepulchre."*
*Canon Pietro Casola's Pilgrimage to Jerusalem,* 182 (quote adapted).

*"And he concluded by saying . . . must enter with Christ in this ship."*
*Canon Pietro Casola's Pilgrimage to Jerusalem,* 179.

*"You want to go to Jerusalem . . . tempests and torments, great storms and winds."*
Guillaume de Deguileville, *The Pilgrimage of Human Life (Le Pèlerinage de la vie humaine),* trans. Eugene Clasby, Garland Library of Medieval Literature 76, ser. B (New York: Garland, 1992), 8.

*"So that we might also have the means to go . . . unless carried over it on the cross of Christ."*

Augustine, *Homilies on the Gospel of John 1–40*, trans. Edmund Hill, ed. Allan D. Fitzgerald, The Works of Saint Augustine 3, no. 12 (Hyde Park, NY: New City, 2009), 56. For more on Augustine and his imagery of the boat, see James K. A. Smith, *On the Road with Saint Augustine: A Real-World Spirituality for Restless Hearts* (Grand Rapids: Brazos, 2019), 14–15.

*"My lords and pilgrims, rise up and come on deck; behold, the land which you long to see is in sight!"*

*The Book of the Wanderings of Brother Felix Fabri*, trans. Aubrey Stewart, vol. I, pt. 1 (London: Palestine Pilgrims' Text Society, 1896), 207 (quote adapted).

## Chapter 8

*"Nevertheless we remained . . . would not let us go on our way."*

*Canon Pietro Casola's Pilgrimage to Jerusalem in the Year 1494*, trans. M. Margaret Newett (Manchester: University Press, 1907), 225 (quote adapted). The terms *Muslim* and *Islam* did not come into general use until the sixteenth century. Consequently, pilgrims like Pietro Casola often use words like *Moor* to describe the inhabitants of the Holy Land. See John V. Tolan, *Saracens: Islam in the Medieval*

*European Imagination* (New York: Columbia University Press, 2002), xv.

*Then Pietro settles on an even more memorable image . . . "as hard as exile and very cruel."*
*Canon Pietro Casola's Pilgrimage to Jerusalem*, 222.

*"I have traveled through nearly all the regions . . . by the dry wind that painful poverty blows."*
Dante Alighieri, *Convivio: A Dual-Language Critical Edition*, ed. and trans. Andrew Frisardi (Cambridge: Cambridge University Press, 2018), 15.

*"Each of us . . . as if we have been cut off from some hidden source of happiness."*
Jen Pollock Michel, *Keeping Place: Reflections on the Meaning of Home* (Downers Grove, IL: IVP, 2017), 27.

*"We all long for [Eden] . . . is still soaked with the sense of 'exile.'"*
*The Letters of J. R. R. Tolkien*, ed. Humphrey Carpenter (New York: Houghton Mifflin Harcourt, 2000), 110.

*"And around the hour of vespers . . . great clarity and beauty, like a star."*
Scott D. Westrem, *Broader Horizons: A Study of Johannes Witte de Hese's* Itinerarius *and Medieval Travel Narratives*, Medieval Academy Books 105 (Cambridge, MA: Medieval Academy of America, 2001), 223.

*Instead, "exile is meant to transform us into pilgrims."*

Michelle Van Loon, *Born to Wander: Recovering the Value of Our Pilgrim Identity* (Chicago: Moody, 2018), 13.

*The poem takes Dante . . . "love that moves the sun and other stars."*

Dante, *The Divine Comedy 3: Paradiso*, trans. and ed. Robin Kirkpatrick (New York: Penguin, 2007), 327.

*In his universal chronicle . . . "into this pilgrimage."*

Otto, Bishop of Freising, *The Two Cities: A Chronicle of Universal History to the Year 1146 A.D.*, trans. Charles Christopher Mierow (New York: Columbia University Press, 2002), 123.

## Chapter 9

*"Nor could I form any idea . . . raise the money for such an expensive journey."*

*The Book of the Wanderings of Brother Felix Fabri*, trans. Aubrey Stewart, vol. I, pt. 1 (London: Palestine Pilgrims' Text Society, 1896), 3.

*"Where shall I get the money . . . friends enough in the various parts of England to help you."*

*The Book of Margery Kempe*, trans. Anthony Bale, Oxford World's Classics (Oxford: Oxford University Press, 2015), 33.

*"The Moors made difficulties . . . we did not want to loosen the sack of money."*

*Canon Pietro Casola's Pilgrimage to Jerusalem in the Year 1494*, trans. M. Margaret Newett (Manchester: University Press, 1907), 225 (quote adapted).

*In 1346, a Franciscan pilgrim . . . or be required to renounce their faith.*

For these two pilgrim stories, see Jonathan Sumption, *The Age of Pilgrimage: The Medieval Journey to God* (Mahwah, NJ: HiddenSpring, 2003; orig. pub. 1975), 265; and Henry L. Savage, "Pilgrimages and Pilgrim Shrines in Palestine and Syria after 1095," in *A History of the Crusades*, vol. 4, *The Art and Architecture of the Crusader States*, ed. Harry W. Hazard (Madison: University of Wisconsin Press, 1977), 44.

*"But the keepers of the gates . . . died of hunger and nakedness."*

Brett Edward Whalen, ed., *Pilgrimage in the Middle Ages: A Reader*, Readings in Medieval Civilizations and Cultures 16 (Toronto: University of Toronto Press, 2011), 184.

*"Just as a true pilgrim . . . you are to make yourself naked of all that you have."*

Walter Hilton, *The Scale of Perfection*, trans. John P. H. Clark and Rosemary Dorward, The Classics of Western Spirituality (New York: Paulist, 1991), 229 (quote adapted).

*"I had to leave behind . . . impede my journey and keep me from reaching Santiago."*

Phileena Heuertz, *Pilgrimage of a Soul: Contemplative Spirituality for the Active Life*, rev. ed. (Downers Grove, IL: IVP, 2017), 88.

*The author of* The Cloud of Unknowing . . . *"simple reaching out to God for himself."*

*The Cloud of Unknowing: With the Book of Privy Counsel*, trans. Carmen Acevedo Butcher (Boston: Shambhala, 2009), 61.

*He describes the necessity . . . acknowledging our poverty and nothingness before God.*

Hilton, *The Scale of Perfection*, 225.

*"These showings make the soul . . . as long as they hold her in their embrace."*

Marguerite Porete, *The Mirror of Simple Souls*, trans. Ellen L. Babinsky, Classics of Western Spirituality (New York: Paulist, 1993), 130 (quote adapted).

*"If you are stripped naked you will be received within."*

Guillaume de Deguileville, *The Pilgrimage of Human Life (Le Pèlerinage de la vie humaine)*, trans. Eugene Clasby, Garland Library of Medieval Literature 76, ser. B (New York: Garland, 1992), 185.

*Francis's biographer, Saint Bonaventure, wrote that he "even took off his underwear."*

Bonaventure, *The Soul's Journey into God, The Tree of Life, The Life of St. Francis*, trans. Ewert Cousins, The Classics of Western Spirituality (Mahwah, NJ: Paulist, 1978), 194.

*"In all things . . . it takes to walk a leisurely mile."*
Bonaventure, *The Soul's Journey into God*, 318 (quote adapted).

*Bonaventure says that Francis instructed the friars . . . "and to travel peacefully."*
Bonaventure, *The Soul's Journey into God*, 241 (emphasis in original; quote adapted).

*"The goal of all spirituality . . . come without title, shame, merit, or even demerit."*
Richard Rohr, "Silence," in Richard's Daily Meditations, Center for Action and Contemplation, August 23, 2012, https://tinyurl.com/ydarjhy9.

*"All we can offer . . . which to all of us never seems like enough."*
Rohr, "Silence."

## Chapter 10

*"Lo, here is the city of the Great King, whose likeness all the Churches of the world are not able to present."*
*John Poloner's Description of the Holy Land (circa 1421 A.D.)*, trans. Aubrey Stewart (London: Palestine Pilgrims' Text Society, 1894), 3.

*"First the stone . . . Then we visited the other places in Jerusalem."*

*The Itineraries of William Wey*, ed. and trans. Francis Davey (Oxford: Bodleian Library, 2010),128–29.

*Here, Felix says, the Savior's footprints . . . "though the print of the right foot is the plainer of the two."*

*The Book of the Wanderings of Brother Felix Fabri*, trans. Aubrey Stewart, vol. I, pt. 2 (London: Palestine Pilgrims' Text Society, 1896), 487.

*"And as fast as the place was emptied he poured more in," marvels Felix.*

*The Book of the Wanderings of Brother Felix Fabri*, vol. 1, pt 2, 487.

*"I, Brother Felix Fabri, did not observe this article strictly, as will appear hereafter."*

*The Book of the Wanderings of Brother Felix Fabri*, vol. I, pt. 1, 249.

*"The keeper of the mosque . . . even had I escaped from the peril of death."*

*The Book of the Wanderings of Brother Felix Fabri*, vol. I, pt. 1, 304 (quote adapted). Like *Moor*, the term *Saracen* was used by fifteenth-century writers to describe the inhabitants of the Holy Land. To many of these writers, *Saracen* meant "pagan" and carried with it connotations of idolatry or heresy. See John V. Tolan, *Saracens: Islam in the Medieval European Imagination* (New York: Columbia University Press, 2002), esp. 127.

*He appears to have made a deal with the two "good-looking, rather tall girls" . . . whenever the girls' father was away.*

*The Book of the Wanderings of Brother Felix Fabri*, vol. II, pt. 1, 138.

*These local guides, she says, "made much of her . . . good and gentle towards her."*

*The Book of Margery Kempe*, trans. Anthony Bale, Oxford World's Classics (Oxford: Oxford University Press, 2015), 70 (quote adapted).

*But Felix also felt frustration . . . praying freely at each one.*

On *The Zion Pilgrim*, see Kathryne Beebe, *Pilgrim and Preacher: The Audiences and Observant Spirituality of Friar Felix Fabri (1437/8–1502)*, Oxford Historical Monographs (Oxford: Oxford University Press, 2014), esp. 109–22.

## Chapter 11

*"Some knelt on the earth . . . that they might endure their thick-coming sobs."*

*The Book of the Wanderings of Brother Felix Fabri*, trans. Aubrey Stewart, vol. I, pt 1 (London: Palestine Pilgrims' Text Society, 1896), 283.

"Oh how joyous an imprisonment! . . . imprisoned in the sepulchre of his Lord!"
The Book of the Wanderings of Brother Felix Fabri, vol. I, pt. 2, 342.

Felix describes the interior as "darksome," with some chapels located underground, "sunk deep among the rocks" . . .
The Book of the Wanderings of Brother Felix Fabri, vol. I, part 2, 352, 361.

The twelfth-century pilgrim Theoderich writes . . . "shines in the church as doth the eye in the head."
Theoderich's Description of the Holy Places (circa 1172 A.D.), trans. Aubrey Stewart (London: Palestine Pilgrims' Text Society, 1891), 19.

Margery writhed and cried out, "for in the city of her soul she saw . . . with pure pity and compassion."
The Book of Margery Kempe, trans. Anthony Bale, Oxford World's Classics (Oxford: Oxford University Press, 2015), 65–66.

From this moment, Margery was graced with "the gift of tears," . . . or "whenever God wished to send them."
The Book of Margery Kempe, trans. Anthony Bale, xvii, 65. Margery also refers to her crying spells as a "well of tears" (91).

"Pay attention, for the base of my cross was set in this hole in the rock at the time of my passion."

*The Revelations of St. Birgitta of Sweden*, Vol. 3, *Liber Cae-lestis, Books VI–VII*, trans. Denis Searby (Oxford: Oxford University Press, 2012), 234.

*"You must direct your attention . . . watch the Crucifixion of our Lord with affection, diligence, love, and perseverance."*

Bonaventure, *The Life of Christ*, trans. and ed. W. H. Hutch-ings (London: Rivingtons, 1881), 248. Although Hutch-ings attributes the text to Bonaventure, we now know that Bonaventure was not the author of the *Meditations* (see full documentation in next entry).

*"Here, then, consider Him diligently . . . you may count yours a heart of stone."*

*Meditations on the Life of Christ: An Illustrated Manu-script of the Fourteenth Century*, trans. and ed. Isa Ragusa and Rosalie B. Green (Princeton, NJ: Princeton University Press, 1961), 329.

*When his group first assembled . . . Felix observed that some of the pilgrims "shrieked as though in labor."*

*The Book of the Wanderings of Brother Felix Fabri*, vol. I, part 1, 283 (quote adapted).

*Metaphorically, "she does give birth to a new Margery, one who cries loudly and uncontrollably when contemplating the sufferings of Jesus."*

Helen Hickey, "Walk This Way: Two Journeys to Jerusalem in the Fifteenth Century," lecture given at *Practising Emo-tions: Place and the Public Sphere*, Uniting Church Theology

College, Parkville, Victoria, Australia, August 7, 2015, https://tinyurl.com/y8d7bhog.

*"I shall go into my own little room . . . and Thee ruling over it."*
Augustine, *Confessions*, trans. Vernon J. Bourke, Fathers of the Church 21 (Washington: Catholic University of America Press, 1966), 385.


Epilogue
*When Friar Felix Fabri departed Jerusalem . . . "like a hospital full of wretched invalids."*
*The Book of the Wanderings of Brother Felix Fabri*, trans. Aubrey Stewart, vol. I, pt 1 (London: Palestine Pilgrims' Text Society, 1896), 24.

*"It requires courage . . . to return to one's home active and well is the especial gift of God."*
*The Book of the Wanderings of Brother Felix Fabri*, vol. I, pt. 1, 47.

*"And when our Lord had brought them back . . . would not travel with her for a hundred pounds."*
*The Book of Margery Kempe*, trans. Anthony Bale, Oxford World's Classics (Oxford: Oxford University Press, 2015), 70.

*"On 30 January 1484 . . . until his brethren had finished and came out to greet his return."*
Kathryne Beebe, *Pilgrim and Preacher: The Audiences and Observant Spirituality of Friar Felix Fabri (1437/8–1502)*, Oxford Historical Monographs (Oxford: Oxford University Press, 2014), 25.

*Felix's brothers at the convent "welcomed him as one come back from the dead."*
*The Book of the Wanderings of Brother Felix Fabri*, vol. II, pt. 2, 676.

*"If you keep on this way, I promise that you shall not be slain but come to the place that you desire."*
Walter Hilton, *The Scale of Perfection*, trans. John P. H. Clark and Rosemary Dorward, The Classics of Western Spirituality (New York: Paulist, 1991), 227 (quote adapted).